WHY REMAIN JEWISH?

David C. Gross

HIPPOCRENE BOOKS
New York

Copyright© 1994 by David C. Gross

For information, contact:
HIPPOCRENE BOOKS, Inc.
171 Madison Avenue
New York, NY 10016

Cataloging-in-Publication Data

Gross, David C., 1923–
    Why remain Jewish? / David C. Gross.
       p.   cm.
    Includes bibliographical references and index.
    ISBN 0-7818-0216-4 :
    1. Judaism—Apologetic works.   2. Judaism—United States.
3. Interfaith marriage—United States.   4. Jews—United States—
Identity.   I. Title.
BM648.G69   1994
296.3—dc20   93-37124
                                                                  CIP

Printed in the United States of America.

CONTENTS

Preface   vii

Chapter I   The Jewish World: A Century of Major Events   1

Chapter II   Is "Jewish" the Same Thing to Everybody?   13

Chapter III   Jews Always Cared for Each Other   25

Chapter IV   In Quest of One's Jewish Identity   37

Chapter V   Only Jews Can Feel Pain of Anti-Semitism   49

Chapter VI   Changing Religions Is a Very Big Step   61

Chapter VII   Is Battle Against Intermarriage Lost?   73

Chapter VIII Hatred's History Looms in
              Shadows   85
Chapter IX   Questions of the Ages vs.
              Intermarriage   97
Chapter X   Certain Families Are More
              Pained Than Others   109
Chapter XI   Do All Parents Really
              Educate Children in
              Judaism?   121
Chapter XII   Did Assimilation Take
              Over for Ambition?   133
Chapter XIII Converts to Judaism
              Have a Message for
              Intermarrieds   145
Chapter XIV   Judaism Is a Tree of Life—
              Hold on to It!   157
Some Useful Addresses   163
Recommended Reading   165
Index   169

PREFACE

What does it mean to title a book *Why Remain Jewish?*

It means that the American Jewish community, the largest in the world, the best-organized and freest, proud of its scholars, rabbis and leaders, generous to a fault to every conceivable Jewish need in the world—this super Jewish community, residing in the greatest democracy in the world, indeed the world's only superpower—this wonderful Jewish community is gradually disintegrating.

There are numerous problems and issues confronting American Jewry: the shallowness of much Jewish religious education for the younger generation, the superficiality of much of American Jewish culture, the poor attendance at synagogue services, the sparsity of a knowledgeable laity.

There is also the problem of a renewed anti-Semitism, both from the extreme right and from segments of the Black population. The cults are a continuing problem, as are aggressive missionaries. The divisiveness among the Orthodox, Conservative and Reform wings of Judaism remain a major issue.

But the one, single, mind-boggling problem that challenges all Jews who care about the continuity of the Jewish people is—intermarriage. If a Jew is a Hasid, and isolates his child from the rest of the world, chances of intermarriage are very slim. If a Jew immigrates to Israel, where 85 per cent of the population is Jewish, again there is only a slight chance that his children will meet non-Jews and intermarry.

But in America—and for that matter, in most western countries—when an educated Jewish young man meets an educated Christian young woman, and they fall in love, inter-marriage often follows. Unless the Gentile partner agrees to convert to Judaism, that little family unit is lost to the Jewish people. The same applies of course to a Jewish young woman and a Gentile young man.

Now, consider the cold facts: The intermarriage figures some 40–50 years ago hovered around five per cent. Today, they already exceed 50 per cent—and the rate is growing. (In isolated Jewish communities, the intermarriage rate is prob-ably above 60 per cent).

At that rate, the Cassandras who predict that American Jewry will in the course of two or three generations fade away may be right. The only exceptions will remain the ultra-Or-thodox and Hasidic sections of the community; although they often appear to be expanding, their numbers compared to the rest of the U.S. Jewish population remain modest.

So, this book *Why Remain Jewish?* is a heartfelt call to all American Jews contemplating intermarriage, to reconsider. Not only for the sake of the Jewish community, and not only so as not to give Hitler a posthumous victory, but for a very personal, subjective reason: I will try to convince you in this volume that being Jewish is very worthwhile, that it is a life-style that will give you and the family you establish great joy and fulfillment, and that being and remaining a Jew will add a vital new dimension to your life, affording you intellectual stimulation, ethical reward, and inner happiness and serenity.

D.C.G.

WHY?

Two Long Island rabbis were asked recently, *Why Remain Jewish?*

One, Ephraim Rubinger, responded by stating that being Jewish is a lifestyle replete with joy and happiness; it is intellectually challenging and ethically rewarding, and that Jews—who have been contributing to society far beyond their numbers for some 4,000 years—will continue to do so in the future. Another reason, he added, is because the chain of Jewish life and history stretches back to the early mists of history, and he did not want to be one of those who would break a link in that chain, thus betraying parents, grandparents and generations of forbears.

Another rabbi, Philmore Berger, said for him being Jewish was worth all the travail that might ensue—combating anti-Semitism, bigotry, the difficult problem of intermarriage—for one primary reason: Judaism believes that this world needs *tikkun,* repairing, improvement, fixing. All of Jewish life focuses on providing succor to the needy, comforting the homeless and sick, providing job opportunities for the unemployed, and most important, ushering in an era of peace for all mankind. This is the principal task of the Jewish people, he said, for Jews throughout history have always shown the way. That is what we were chosen to do.

Chapter I

The Jewish World: A Century of Major Events

THE JEWISH WORLD—THE JEWISH PEOPLE, THE JEWISH RELI-
gion, all aspects of Jewish life—have been turned topsy turvy
in the last century. For nearly two thousand years Jews in
nearly every corner of the world prayed and dreamed and
hoped that their ancient homeland would be rebuilt, and that
they would return there and resume their lives as citizens of a
restored Jewish state. What happened?

In 1948, the State of Israel was proclaimed, and threw its

doors wide open to all Jews. One of Israel's first laws said that every Jew who came home would automatically and instantly become a citizen. So, some 300,000 survivors of the Holocaust flooded into Israel, destitute, broken in body and in spirit, and began to rebuild their lives. Tens of thousands of other Holocaust survivors—who had miraculously lived through the Nazi death camps and ghettos—preferred to settle in the United States, in western Europe, or Australia. And incredible as it may seem, small numbers even preferred to remain in Germany, Poland and Austria.

In Israel's early years, Jews who had lived in Moslem countries for many centuries—Libya, Syria, Iraq, Morocco, Yemen and other lands—proceeded en masse and under duress to Israel. Their erstwhile neighbors coveted what little the Jews had, made life uncomfortable for them, and so the Jews from these non-European countries arrived in Israel. All told, they numbered 800,000.

From the free countries, the United States, Britain, France, Holland, Latin America and Italy, there was a steady flow of idealistic immigrants, Jews who believed that the rebirth of Israel was an historic event of enormous proportions. They wished to link their lives to the old-new homeland, and to sink roots into the ancient soil. Their numbers were not great but the contribution they made to the country's development was disproportionately high.

The establishment of Israel continues to have a tremendous impact on the Jewish community in all sectors of the world.

But that is only a part of the story. One hundred years ago the overwhelming majority of European Jews lived in eastern Europe—in Poland, Russia, Lithuania, Romania and the surrounding areas. The Jews who lived in England, France, Germany and the United States were largely different from their east European coreligionists. By and large the east European Jews were Orthodox, a great many were Hasidic, and their lives centered around the synagogue, the cycle of Jewish holidays, and the Sabbath that culminated each week. In the western countries, the Enlightenment movement and the cultures of the surrounding people among whom they lived had transformed the Jews—they had begun to lead lives that were becoming indistinguishable from those of their neighbors.

Instances of assimilation and intermarriage were not uncommon in the United States, England and other western lands; in Germany, and to a lesser extent in France, large numbers of Jews believed that to survive, to get ahead, to succeed, the only path that made sense was to become baptized, and to join the Church. The great poet Heinrich Heine did precisely that, and then deeply regretted it. One of modern Jewry's greatest philosophers and theologians, Franz Rosenzweig, almost took the same step, and then pulled back. He became instead a seminal Jewish thinker and an Orthodox spokesman.

In 1890, millions of Jews lived in eastern Europe; the families of many of them had resided in the same towns and cities for hundreds of years. The Jewish population of Poland traced its origins back 1,000 years. In America, there were relatively small numbers of Jews, most of them either from Germany, a country they had fled in the middle of the nineteenth century, or descendants of the Sephardim, Jews who originated in the Mediterranean Sea area but who had been expelled, largely to Holland and England, and had eventually made their way to the United States.

There were also a small number of Jewish settlers living in Turkish-controlled Palestine, a slim piece of land in the Turkish Empire's vast holdings. By and large these settlers were idealistic agricultural workers who hoped that one day many more thousands would join them and reestablish the old-new homeland.

Jewish scholarship and leadership were centered in eastern Europe. In Lithuania and Poland there were vast numbers of yeshivot—all-day Jewish academies—where students devoted their lives to the study of the great texts of Judaism—the Hebrew Bible, the Talmud, and in some cases the mystical Kabalah. Whatever Jewish schools existed in the western countries were at that time on a far lower cultural level. When a synagogue in the United States found itself in need of a rabbi or a cantor or a qualified religious teacher, in those years they

generally turned to the great institutions in Poland and
Lithuania.

In the 1990s, the situation of the Jewish people has been
turned upside down and sideways. The millions of Jews who
lived in the Soviet Union in the wake of the Communist take-
over were barred from studying anything that touched on Judaism. The Hebrew language was banned. Bibles were
outlawed. Jewish customs, traditions, prayers, rituals, holidays were all ripped out of the heart of this once-great community. Although Poland was not formally part of the Soviet
Union, as were Lithuania and Ukraine where the bulk of the
Jewish population lived, anti-Semitic, xenophobic regimes
through the years made life for the Jews difficult although liv-
able . . . until 1939, when the Nazis invaded and within a
few short years massacred more than three million Polish
Jews—a community that before World War II made up one-
tenth of the Polish population.

In the 1990s, the United States is the center of the world's
Jews, with a population of a little less than six million; Israel
has become the second largest Jewish community, with a Jewish population exceeding four million, while the Jews remaining in Russia, following the collapse of the Soviet Union,
and the former Soviet lands are estimated to total between one
and two million. (The fourth largest Jewish community in the
world is found in France; the community's size grew after the
French-dominated North African countries were cut off from
the French government, and many Jews proceeded either to Israel or to France.)

A visitor to the United States from, say Sweden or Chile,
could be forgiven if he looks about him, and—as a Jew from a
tiny community—marvels at the American Jewish community.

"More than three thousand synagogues!" he will exclaim.

"The colleges and universities teach Hebrew and Judaic
studies!"

"In certain neighborhoods, men and boys walk around
wearing yarmulkes, unafraid and proud!"

"The supermarkets are filled with food that is strictly kosher!"

"On the major Jewish holidays, many public schools close because so many teachers stay home!"

"Why are you American Jews so worried about the future? You have several rabbinical seminaries, you have hundreds of yeshivot, you have hundreds of thousands of Jewish boys and girls studying in Jewish religious schools, you have so many organizations raising funds for the sick and needy, for Jewish education, for settling new immigrants in Israel, for help to the Israeli universities, for so many wonderful causes. Why are you concerned?"

Why?

There are today more than a half-million Jewish young men and women studying at American colleges and universities. There is no doubt that our community is highly educated, but of that half-million enrollment more than half of that figure—250,000—is destined to intermarry, assimilate and for all intents and purposes be lost to the Jewish community. Chances are high that they will marry fine, intelligent spouses of the Christian faith, have fine, intelligent children and these children will no longer be Jewish.

To put it another way: The biggest challenge confronting the American Jewish community today is not anti-Semitism but intermarriage, assimilation and disappearance from the Jewish community.

As if intermarriage were not enough of a challenge facing American Jews, additional numbers of young Jews are being lost to the Jewish people as a result of the efforts of Christian missionaries and cults of various kinds. One survey estimated that the number of Jews—young men and women in their twenties and thirties, in most cases—who have abandoned Judaism and the Jewish people for a cultic group has already passed the 100,000 mark.

A thoughtful, sensitive person, Jew or Gentile, particularly one who has just visited the Holocaust Museum in Washington and has seen the grim truth about the destruction of six million European Jews by the Nazis and their collaborators, might muse: If more Jews are being lost to intermarriage, and to the cults and missionaries, then it is as though Hitler is enjoying a posthumous victory.

One tries to be understanding and compassionate. A friend's son brings along a lovely young lady to a family celebration. "She's not Jewish," you are told, "and she's not converting." You talk with her, and you like her immediately. She is wise, witty, gentle, educated. She will make some lucky fellow a good wife, but this particular young man—if he marries her—will give up his identity, his background, his traditions. One doubts he will ever take on her family's culture and customs and ways. He will simply remain in limbo all his life, neither here nor there. I try to understand his head, and put myself in his shoes. He never had much of a Jewish family tradition at home. For a brief time, before his bar mitzvah, his parents were members of the synagogue, and then they dropped out. For Passover, he came to our house for the seder.

If this really fine young man were to ask me, Why? Why should I remain Jewish? How would I respond?

I can just hear him saying to me, "There is so much anti-Semitism in the world—of course I know it's insane—but who needs it? Life is short, it's meant to be enjoyed, there's so much I'd like to do and see, who needs an extra hassle?"

Or he might say: "Look, you know I'm ambitious, I want to get ahead—if they close the best clubs or schools to Jews, they're a bunch of stupid bigots. I can outsmart them, don't you see? If they ask me what church I go to, I can say Presbyterian or Episcopalian. It's none of their business, of course, but it's—to me—a little white lie. It doesn't mean a thing."

Oh, no?

What about all the people in the world today who are searching for their roots, their identity? Isn't it clear that something very basic is missing if a grown man or woman digs deeply to learn who were the grandparents, the great grandparents, the place of origin? If people are a product of both "nature and nurture" then it follows that every person's genes are important, and to walk away from one's true heritage is an act of great folly. And maybe worse.

For every person who is asking, clearly or subconsciously, *Why should I remain Jewish? Why should I continue to be a part of this persecuted people, when it seems so easy just to slip away? Let me weigh the pluses and the minuses, and then decide for myself.*

Answering that question is the primary purpose of writing this book. It is, I confess, not an easy answer to come up with, but the answer is there, it is meaningful, and hopefully this book will persuade some, perhaps many, young Jews contemplating intermarriage to reconsider.

There isn't a single Jewish family in America today—with the probable exception of the Hasidic group—that isn't aware of someone close who is married to a Gentile who rejects conversion. Examples abound:

- One man I know, himself a Holocaust survivor, has three sons. One son married a Jewish girl, another married a Gentile girl who converted (and is therefore considered fully Jewish—no ifs, ands or buts), and the third boy married a Gentile girl who declined the suggestion that she convert. Each son and wife now have children, and thus there are Jewish grandchildren and Gentile grandchildren. My friend looks at me, and says a little sheepishly, "What can I do?" He loves all the grandchildren but during the Christmas holiday season (and Easter) he feels cut off from his Christian grandchildren, and from his son, their father. Of course they all come to the Passover seder, and enjoy together, but the Gentile daughter-in-law acts uncomfortable, and her children feel out of place as their Jewish cousins belt out the traditional holiday songs.

  To all intents and purposes that Jewish father-husband is lost to the Jewish people. His parents have never asked him whether he attends church with his wife and children. They don't want to know.

- A neighbor's boy, a family friend for decades, moved 3,000 miles away from home to take a job. He met a lovely young woman, who found the idea of conversion appalling, they got married, and at last count have two children. That boy is lost to the Jewish community, notwithstanding the fact that his wife may be a marvelous person and the children turn out beautifully.

- A lovely young Jewish girl from a traditional, religious family got married. Things did not work out, so they got divorced. She too moved some 3,000 miles away. She found a good job, tried to put her life together by meeting an eligible Jewish young man, failed to meet someone suitable but met, in her office, a very eligible Christian man. Despite her family's objections, they married—a religious Jewish woman and a Christian man. They now have a child, who according to Jewish religious law is Jewish (because the mother is Jewish) but that little girl will receive two distinct, separate heritages, one from Judaism and one from Christianity. Whether she will grow up to become a Jewish woman who will marry a Jew and establish a Jewish family is questionable.
- A Jewish young man, a social worker, the product of a broken family, met a Gentile girl, they fell in love and married. They now have a child, and the father has agreed to the child's being educated in a Catholic school. His siblings and mother suspect that he has formally converted to Catholicism, although he has kept that secret.

There was a survey of the American Jewish community recently to try to determine the exact numbers of the community which once exceeded six million (at that time about 3 per cent of the American population, and today down to about 2½ per cent). The demographic study was not successful because those questioned as to whether they were Jewish said yes, but in a great many cases Jewish religious law does not regard them as bona fide Jews. For example: Orthodox and Conservative Judaism count a child's religious affiliation by the religion of the mother; thus, if the mother is Jewish, so is the child. In Reform Judaism, children born to a Jewish father who says he will raise the child as a Jew is also considered a Jew—but this definition is rejected by the other two mainstreams of American Judaism. Then there are cases where a Jewish woman is divorced and later remarried—without first obtaining a religious divorce, known as a get. Orthodox and Conservative Jews would not consider her children (from the second husband) Jewish, unless the children were converted.

Thus, with the best of intentions, it is easy to see how Jewish families who are ignorant of Jewish law can easily fall by the wayside, and without wishing to, drop out of the Jewish community.

The great Jewish historian Cecil Roth once estimated that the Jewish people, one of the oldest, continuing peoples in the world, would today easily number more than 100 million if— if there had been no pogroms, no expulsions, no forced conversions, no massacres.

The demographics of the Jewish people are an important factor. Although it is true that at one time, several centuries ago when infants did not often live beyond a few days or weeks, there were only one million Jews in the world, the fact is that in the summer of 1939, just before the Nazis launched World War II, there were some 18 million Jews in the world. When the war ended, there were 12 million. To their credit, the Orthodox Jewish families do have large families, as do the Sephardic families in Israel, but by and large American Jewish families do not. One or two children seem to be the norm in the Jewish community in the United States, a figure that will not even maintain the 12 million Jews in the world today.

In other words, the challenge in American Jewry consists not only of intermarriage, assimilation and disappearance, but when a Jewish couple does get married, they either have no children or settle for one or two. Is it any wonder that some Cassandras predict that the American Jewish community will shrink to one million or even less in a matter of two or three more generations?

I can just see a dissenting reader raise his hand. "Author!" he is shouting. "Wait a minute. What about all those people who are converting to Judaism?"

Good question. Let's tackle it and respond. Yes, there are Christian converts to Judaism. Some even estimate as many as ten thousand annually in the United States alone. No one really knows for sure. Many converts do so because they are sincerely religious, they have made a serious study of Judaism, contrasted it with other faiths, and have decided that that is the religion they wish to affiliate with. Fine. This is not new in Jewish history. In Czarist Russia there was a member of the aristocracy, a count, who became a Jew; in the United States, there was once a well-known newspaper columnist who chose Judaism (in fact the converts like to call themselves *Jews by Choice*). In Israel there is a bearded, Orthodox rabbi married to the daughter of Holocaust survivors who is himself a convert—from German Catholicism. His father was a member of the Nazi army.

Most converts in the United States, however, decide to take that step because they are in love, and the Jewish man or woman has made it clear that the conversion is a first step toward marriage. Most such conversions seem to be successful, and a great many of the woman converts often turn out to be far more observant of Jewish laws and tradition than do born Jews.

But—and this is the problem: More than half of all marriages entered into by a Jew today in the United States is with a non-Jew. Most of these Jewish men or women in such an intermarriage do not formally convert to Christianity, nor do they formally renounce Judaism. Indeed, many if not most assure their parents that the children will be raised as Jews, even though they themselves hardly know anything about Judaism. These mixed couples will come to family seders at Passover time, and to wedding and bar or bat mitzvah receptions.

But the cold, hard fact is that no matter how wonderful the Gentile partner in the marriage is, no matter how warm and friendly the Gentile partner's family is to the Jewish family involved in the intermarriage, this will no longer really be a Jewish family. It will be another loss to the Jewish community in the United States.

In most synagogue membership rules there is a bylaw that

states that intermarried families may join the congregation, but only the Jewish partner in the marriage may be honored by being called to the Torah, opening the ark where the Torah scrolls are kept, and the like. Which of course must make the non-Jewish partner feel like an outsider.

I once saw the son of an intermarried family called to the Torah for his bar mitzvah. I knew the father was Jewish, and the mother was not. The boy came up to the raised platform with his father; both were wearing the traditional prayer shawls, and the young man proceeded to recite his assigned biblical portion, his father standing alongside him proudly. When the reading was concluded, the young man approached the rabbi, and the father stood a little to the side. The rabbi asked the mother, who was in the congregation with her young daughter, to rise so that he could bless the bar mitzvah boy and the family. She rose, remained standing for a moment, and then dashed out of the synagogue in tears. In her mind, the blessing and the bar mitzvah ceremony seemed to stamp her son's Jewishness forever—and she simply could not handle it.

It turned out that apparently the parents had agreed to raise their son as a Jew and their daughter as a Catholic, but the bar mitzvah ceremony and the actuality of seeing her son encased in a new *tallit* (prayer shawl) were too much for the mother. Later, rumors circulated that the couple decided to divorce.

In other words, when there is a conversion to Judaism that is sincere, it is usually a positive step for the Jewish community. Numerically, however, compared with the numbers of Jews who intermarry, the Jews lose. If more than half of all marriages involving a Jewish partner is with a non-Jew who has no intention of converting to Judaism, the number of Jews in the United States will continue to decline. There simply are no two ways about it.

This question of *Why Remain Jewish?* is not at all new. There have been Jews in the long history of the Jewish people who have espoused voluntary assimilation believing that it would finally put an end to anti-Semitism. There are also Jews who wish to remain secular Jews, cutting off all contact with religion, maintaining that Jewish music, dance, art and culture should be separated from what they see as outdated religious practice that is out of tune with the twentieth century.

The late Rabbi Meir Kahane, who was an extremist in his political views, was also a strongly committed Orthodox Jew, who felt that Judaism, without strict observance of the laws and traditions, was empty. His philosophy has caught on with those Jews who in their twenties and thirties have decided to become ultra-Orthodox, and to devote their lives to Jewish religious study. These young men (and some women) are the *Baalei T'shùvah;* there aren't really that many of them, but they come from the United States, England and Israel, and are generally to be seen in the religious areas of Jerusalem, or in certain sections of New York or London. They seem to be following Kahane's teachings, as well as those of other traditionalists. In 1977, Kahane said:

Judaism lives or dies on the unique fact that God revealed Himself at Mount Sinai and gave the Jew a truth that no one else has. Judaism lives or dies on the fact that the Bible and the Talmud with their laws, commandments, statutes and ordinances were divinely revealed and that the only way to holiness and true goodness comes from the observance of Torah laws.

His interpretation opens up the word "Jewish" in the question *"Why Remain Jewish?"* There are, as an intelligent reader can quickly discern, differing interpretations of the Jewish religion and Jewish life.

Chapter II

Is "Jewish" the Same Thing to Everybody?

MANY JEWS THINK OF THEMSELVES AS PROUD JEWS. "BEING Jewish is very important to me," they'll say, although if you pin them down they will often admit that they do not support a synagogue, are not members of any Jewish organization, do not read Jewish newspapers, magazines or books, have never visited Israel, and hardly celebrate any of the Jewish holidays. Then what do they mean?

Probably that they share in the achievements of world-famous Jewish scientists and artists, or perhaps that they are ready at a moment's notice to punch the nose of a virulent anti-Semite. Or perhaps—and this is often the case—they are nostalgia Jews: They remember the Jewish dishes that a mother or grandmother served them, and they seek out a Jewish-style restaurant to savor some of the old tastes.

Thus, logically, before one can answer the question, *Why Remain Jewish?*, one must get a good grip on the word "Jewish"—what does it really mean? The Israeli government, from time to time, in its efforts to determine who is entitled to receive automatic citizenship has struggled with the problem of Who Is a Jew? Religious leaders, from the extreme right and all shades in between leading to the left, have expressed widely different viewpoints on that question. In the early years of Israel's statehood, when the question arose during the prime ministership of David Ben Gurion, he gave a quick response which has been shunted aside. The Israeli leader said: Anyone who calls himself a Jew is Jewish. But the rabbis said no; there are certain rules and regulations, and they must be adhered to. To some extent the question still remains unanswered because not all Jews freely accept the decisions of the rabbinical authorities. It remains a complex issue.

The United States senator from Connecticut, Joseph I. Lieberman, an Orthodox Jew, was asked recently to respond to the question, What Being Jewish Means to Me. This is what he said:

> To me, being Jewish means having help in life's most fundamental questions, such as, "How did I come to this place?" and "Now that I am here, how should I live?"
>
> My faith, which has anchored my life, begins with a joyful gratitude that there is a God who created the universe and then, because He continued to care for what He created, gave us laws and values to order and improve our lives. God also gave us a purpose and a destiny—to do justice and to protect, indeed to perfect, the human community and natural environment.
>
> In trying to live according to these principles, I am helped by daily prayer and religious rituals such as observance of the Sabbath—a time to stop and appreciate all that God has given us. I also find strength and humility in being linked to something so much larger and longer-lasting than myself.
>
> Being Jewish in America also means feeling a special love for

this country, which has provided such unprecedented freedom and opportunity to the millions who have come and lived here. My parents raised me to believe that I did not have to mute my religious faith or ethnic identity to be a good American, that, on the contrary, America invites all its people to be what they are and believe what they wish. In truth, it is from our individual diversity and shared faith in God that we Americans draw our greatest strength and hope.

Almost every Jew has a different idea of what being Jewish is. There are for example American Jews who do not observe the Sabbath, do not eat kosher foods, and yet when they visit Israel they become hopping mad—they want every Israeli to be strictly religious and follow all the rules that he himself ignores. (The degree of religiosity in Israel coincides more or less with that of the Jewish community in the U.S.)

There are also some Jews who become embarrassed, perhaps even fearful, if they hear Jewish jokes on television that seem to them offensive, or loud. It is a common Jewish failing: we wish to appear to be as honest, as positive, as righteous as possible, and if someone spoils that public image, many of us become upset.

In other words, American Jews really lead two separate and distinct lives: one life is outside, at work, among our Gentile friends, colleagues and neighbors. A second life is inside the home—where we can let our barriers down, relax, and poke fun at ourselves if we wish.

Almost from childhood on, we are advised and taught: To thine own self be true. It is a wonderful maxim, but, sad to say, when it comes to one's own identity, Jews very often try to appear as "non-Jewish" as possible—to advance their careers, to be one of the boys, not to rock the boat. It is a fact that for American Jews over the age of fifty, memory of their lives a half-century ago—here, in the United States—has remained a painful experience.

It may be hard to believe, in the 1990s and on the eve of the 21st century, but some 50 years ago Jews were barred from employment in banks, in utilities, in insurance companies.

These were known as Gentile fields. What is more, the employment ads stated clearly and boldly: Jews need not apply.

In this same period, American Jews can remember that the universities and colleges all around the country, including the Ivy League institutions, practiced a form of restrictive discrimination. They simply did not want to have "too many" Jewish students, and blatantly barred them when they applied. Many a would-be Jewish physician was thus forced to pursue his medical studies in Italy, Germany (before the Nazi rise to power in 1933), England and elsewhere.

Someone once said that being Jewish is like belonging to a great, big family and familial closeness is not always a pleasant fact of life. All too often, members of a family argue, stop talking to one another, criticize sharply. Like all minorities in the United States, the Jews take great pride in the achievements of fellow Jews; and when a Jew is arrested or indicted for a crime, most of us hide our heads in shame.

I remember once sitting in a coffee shop with my wife in a hotel in Zurich, Switzerland. The Swiss, by and large, are a polite, quiet people. We were having our dinner when the door opened and a couple walked in. He was talking loudly, with what I was sure was a heavy Yiddish accent, steering his guest to a table directly behind us. He could be heard all over the restaurant, almost shouting, his actions making me wince. Mind you, I was never sure that he was a Jew but to my sensitive eye and ear, he seemed to be—and that was enough. After some ten minutes I deliberately turned my chair around, faced him, and stared him in the eye. I suppose I tried to convey an ESP message which said, "Quiet! You loud fool!" He looked at me once, did not get the message, and continued his accented loud speech. As soon as possible, we finished eating, paid the check and left. The incident upset me for a few days.

I suppose that there is one very enjoyable perk most Jewish tourists receive when they go to Israel. This is a Jewish country, everyone can be themselves; they can speak gently or roughly, as they wish. More than one Jewish visitor to Israel has made the same comment: When they get to Israel they feel as though the psychological weights that they carry about them nearly all the time "over there," in the non-Jewish world, have been lifted. They can relax and, perhaps more than ever, be themselves. The psychological pressures of being a minority in a majority culture disappear the moment they land in Israel, and as soon as they return to America, to their home, they sense the return of those pressures. All of this, of course, is part of being Jewish.

Is it any wonder that some younger members of the Jewish community wonder, either aloud, or in their heart of hearts, *Why Remain Jewish?* Why do I need this extra burden in my life? Is it worth it? This book's answer is a resounding yes. It is very, very much worth the effort, but please don't just take my word for it. You decide; weigh the pluses and minuses. It is, as they say, your life.

Rosalyn Yalow, the 1977 Nobel Laureate in Medicine, was also asked What Being Jewish Means to Me. This is what she replied:

As a Jew I share a strong commitment to the Jewish intellectual tradition. That tradition places emphasis on learning—learning for the sake of understanding and perfecting our world, and learning for its own sake. Through the ages we have taken pride in being known as the "People of the Book" and have carried our Torah and our traditions with dignity and affection. Even in the face of persecution and dispersion, and often denied access to centers of learning, the Jewish people, never satisfied with conventional answers, have always valued intellectual inquiry and continued to honor wisdom and learning.

Moreover, being Jewish means to me having a deep attachment to family. I grew up in an era of tightly-knit families which shaped our values and world-view. Today, the family, including the Jewish family, is said to be an endangered institution. It is time for us to rededicate ourselves to strengthening Jewish family life. Surely this is our best investment in the Jewish future.

Finally, Judaism represents a great synthesis of universal and Jewish values. For me as a Jew, there need be no conflict between science and religion. Moses Maimonides, philosopher and codifier of Halachah (Jewish law), also graced the world of medicine. He is a role model of living in two worlds, Jewish and universal, and of making them one.

The greatness of this country is that here we can be fully Jewish and fully American. American Jews are blessed to be living in a country where one need not compromise one's Jewishness to enjoy the opportunities of an open, pluralistic society.

In a world that is too often concerned with instant pleasures and self-gratification, Jews have long believed in the importance of scholarship and disciplined learning. Accordingly, let us rededicate ourselves to the traditional values of our people and the service of humanity.

In the aftermath of the Holocaust, one hears stories of survivors who reacted to that obscene experience in vastly different ways. Two young Jewish children in Belgium, who were rescued by the kindness and courage of a convent, were reunited with their relatives when World War II ended. One, the boy, threw himself into studying Judaism and in the course of time immigrated to Israel, became an observant Jew and to this day works for the government.

The other child, his sister, had become accustomed to life in a convent and to Catholic teaching. She opted to formally adopt Catholicism and lives today in Belgium, a married woman with children; her husband is a fellow Catholic. Once or twice a year her Jewish brother visits her from Jerusalem. There are innumerable stories like these that came out of the Holocaust—Jewish survivors who had been sheltered by Christians who chose to remain Christian, and at the same time others who survived the horrible Nazi period and quickly resumed their identities and lives as Jews.

One such survivor arrived in New York soon after the end of World War II, altered his name so that it sounded non-Jewish, married a Gentile woman whom he did not tell that he was of Jewish extraction, and together they had two daughters, whom they raised totally without any religious affiliation whatsoever. They lived for some twenty-five years in a suburb of New York that was known to be virtually without any Jewish residents. And thus, for the major part of his life, this man hid his Jewish origins, never told his wife or daughters, or friends and neighbors. To all intents and purposes, he was a religious neuter—until he died.

An envelope was found among his papers after he died which was marked, "To Be Opened at My Death." The family opened the envelope and read with shock and amazement his confession that he had hidden his Jewishness from everyone virtually all his life, primarily he explained because he was afraid of anti-Semitism, and that he had one final request: he wished to be buried in a Jewish cemetery. Enclosed in the envelope was a deed to a burial plot in a Jewish cemetery on Long Island.

Can one even begin to imagine the daily anguish that that man lived through as he covered up his identity?

Contrast his identity reaction with another Holocaust survivor, Elie Wiesel, the Nobel Laureate who won the prize for peace in 1986 and who of course is world-known for his lifelong dedication to recounting the Holocaust, so that such an obscenity might never recur. He too was asked to respond to the question, What Being Jewish Means to Me. This is what he said:

> I remember, as a child, on the other side of oceans and mountains, the Jew in me would anticipate Rosh Hashanah with fear and trembling. He still does.
>
> On that Day of Awe, I believed then, nations and individuals, Jewish and non-Jewish, are being judged by their common creator. That is still my belief.
>
> In spite of all that happened? Because of all that happened!
>
> I still believe that to be Jewish today means what it meant yesterday and a thousand years ago. It means for the Jew in me to seek fulfillment both as a Jew and as a human being. For a Jew, Judaism and humanity must go together. To be Jewish today is to recognize that every person is created in the image of God and that our purpose in living is to be a reminder of God.
>
> Naturally I claim total kinship with my people and its destiny. Judaism integrates particularist aspirations with universal values, fervor with rigor, legend with law. Being Jewish for me is to reject all fanaticism anywhere.

To be Jewish is, above all, to safeguard memory and open its gates to the celebration of life as well as to the suffering, to the song of ecstasy as well as to the tears of distress that are our legacy as Jews. It is to rejoice in the renaissance of Jewish sovereignty in Israel and the re-awakening of Jewish life in the former Soviet Union. It is to identify with the plight of Jews living under oppressive regimes and with the challenges facing our communities in free societies.

A Jew must be sensitive to the suffering of all human beings. A Jew cannot remain indifferent to human suffering, whether in former Yugoslavia, in Somalia, or in our own cities and towns. The mission of the Jewish people has never been to make the world more Jewish, but to make the world more human.

In the 1920s, shortly after the end of World War I, when the automobile was beginning to impact on the world, when flappers were all the rage in New York, Paris and London, when the stock market was beginning its meteoric rise and almost everyone thought millionaires would soon abound in every nook and cranny of the western world, a young Jewish intellectual, an academic in Paris, was trying to make up his mind: Should he convert and become a Catholic or not?

Edmond Fleg remembered that his grandfather had been a pious, gentle man but his own parents had neglected to give him a serious, meaningful Jewish religious education. To succeed in university life in France, and perhaps to go on to high positions in the government's education ministry, it was almost essential to be a Roman Catholic.

But, he reasoned, before he took the awesome step of changing his religious affiliation he would look into Judaism, about which he felt he knew nothing, and see just exactly what it was he was giving up. Well, what happened could almost have been predicted. Fleg was a highly intelligent person, and he found that the more he read in Jewish texts and the more he considered Judaism's basic teachings, the more convinced he became that renouncing Judaism would be a grave error. Indeed, he recalled, he felt like an explorer—he had found in Judaism a faith that he had been searching for, an intellectual faith, and one in which the sages of old taught that *not* to question was the height of folly.

He quickly canceled all plans to convert and instead began to observe more and more Jewish religious laws, all the time enlarging his knowledge and understanding of Judaism's laws and traditions. In 1927, he wrote a short book, ostensibly addressed to his unborn grandson, titled *Why I Am a Jew,* which became a popular book in the 1930s in the United States.

Fleg wrote that "I am a Jew because the faith of Israel demands no abdication of the mind . . . I am a Jew because in all places where there are tears and suffering the Jew weeps . . . I am a Jew because the message of Israel is the most ancient and the most modern . . . I am a Jew because Israel's promise is a universal promise. . . . I am a Jew because for Israel the world is not finished, men will complete it."

Fleg describes a visit to a museum in Geneva. First he sees a depiction of the Geneva synagogue's door "through which my father entered to pray." Then he views a bridge over the Rhine, wondering if his grandfather crossed there; he wonders also if his grandfather was a kabbalist and calculated the mystical numbers found in Hebrew letters. And "the grandfather of the grandfather of his grandfather—perhaps he was a weigher of gold in the Amsterdam ghetto, painted by Rembrandt." Fleg muses on:

"One of my ancestors may have drunk from that wine cup (in the museum) upon returning home after listening to the teaching of his master, Rashi, in the School of Troyes in Champagne. One of my ancestors may have sat in that armchair studded with jade when a sultan bade him feel his pulse; one of my ancestors may have seen his children crushed beneath the hooves of the Crusader's horse, the horseman bearing all that armor."

By and large, Jews feel comfortable with one another. No matter how many generations they have lived in America, no matter how well they have assimilated into American social or business life, when they are together they feel more at ease.

The former president of Israel, Chaim Herzog, a lawyer by

profession, likes to tell about a time when he was in Taiwan on business. It was evening and he was sitting in the Taipeh hotel lobby, relaxing, and looking at the widely variegated people who passed by. Suddenly he heard an announcement on the public address system, with the young lady's mild Chinese accent wafting through the hotel. She called out:

"Wanted! Wanted! In room 865, one more for minyan, one more for minyan." Herzog smiled, rose and took the elevator to the eighth floor, to room 865. And there he found nine Jewish men, waiting for him, the tenth. A minyan is a religious quorum needed for a prayer service. One of the men in the room wished to recite the mourner's prayer, the kaddish, and Herzog's arrival made it possible. He was given a yarmulke, and the service began. He remembered later that there were Israelis, Americans, Australians and a Frenchman in the room, all Jews.

Similar incidents take place relatively frequently. Some years ago an international scientific conference was being held in Geneva. In the middle of the addresses, the simultaneous translation system broke down. The chairman looked about him, unsure of himself. Then he spoke into the microphone. "Please raise your hand if you understand English," he said. A few hands went up. He tried again. "Francais?" Again a few hands went up. Then suddenly he had a brainstorm. "Yiddish?" A roomful of delegates raised their hands, and for a while that world scientific gathering carried on in Yiddish, until the translation system was repaired.

A friend of mine recently took a cruise on the Carribean. Everything was very pleasant, and somewhat formal since almost everyone was a stranger to one another. One morning my friend put on a T-shirt that he had received as a gift. It bore the word "Harvard" in Hebrew letters. (He had never had an opportunity to go to college). As he paraded around the deck, passengers greeted him warmly; some said they could make out the word, others asked what it meant. The ice was broken. My friend always carries a prayer book with him, and although there was no formal Sabbath eve (Friday night) service scheduled to take place on board, he decided to try.

He photocopied several pages from his prayer book, and ran off enough copies for twenty people. He posted a notice on the bulletin board about the service; one of the passengers approached him and said he was a rabbi's son and would like to lead the service. When the time arrived, some 70 people showed up. The men wore all kinds of makeshift hats; a handful had yarmulkes. The rabbi's son conducted the service beautifully, and there, on the ocean blue, a Jewish religious service took place that all found inspiring and memorable.

And to everyone's surprise and delight, the ship's captain arranged for traditional wine and a challah to help usher in the Sabbath.

If among the passengers there had also been a Jew who was denying his identity, can one imagine his chagrin and anguish and confusion?

To thine own self be true.

I was once invited to lunch in midtown New York, at the town house home of a multimillionaire, a Gentile. We were four at the table—the host, his son-in-law (also a Gentile), the host's long-time Jewish lawyer, and me. There was a private dining room, a private kitchen, and of course a waiter. I was seated alongside the lawyer, facing the other two people. From the corner of my eye I saw the waiter emerge from the kitchen bearing four plates, on each of which was a hefty ham and cheese sandwich. I was the last to be served. As the waiter approached, I asked him, in a whisper, to please remove the ham.

My host, a man from the south in his advanced years, known throughout the country for his politically conservative views, stared at me for a moment, and then slammed hard on the table. We could all see and hear the dishes and silver rattle.

"By God," the host shouted, "I respect a man who respects his religion!" I didn't know what to say, and said nothing. I did however feel sorry for the lawyer seated next to me; he seemed to be choking on the sandwich.

To hold one's head high every day, to look into the mirror

and never feel ashamed for anything that we have done, to know in one's heart that we are going through life doing good deeds, not hiding our identity, not pretending we are someone else, feeling inwardly at ease and at peace—this is clearly a wonderful way to live.

For a Jewish person, to live this kind of a clean-cut, open life is especially important since all too many Jews know so little of their religious tradition; it may seem at times expedient for some to try to get off the Jewish bandwagon. Such a step, such an attitude spells great danger, and can lead to disastrous results. The poor Jewish souls caught up in the cults, or who fall prey to the missionaries, or the large numbers who intermarry without realizing the consequences to their future lives and to their very peace of mind need to be cautioned: If you wish to abandon Judaism and the Jewish people, that is your right—but, please, for your sake, first learn something about your heritage before you cut it out of your life. Any other step can be spiritually suicidal.

Chapter III

Jews Always Cared for Each Other

ONE OF THE VILEST, AND MOST PREPOSTEROUS ANTI-SEMITIC diatribes ever concocted against Jews, is the notorious "Protocols of the Elders of Zion." A document faked during the days of repressive Czarist anti-Semitism at the turn of the century, it alleges that there exists an international cabal of diabolically clever Jews who seek to control the world through manipulating the media, the banks, the stock market—and that when their super-secret plot to do so succeeds, Jews will take control of the whole world. The fact that the documents were forged was proven almost from the day they first appeared. Nonetheless, Nazis and Arab fanatics as well as anti-Semites of various other stripes continue to publish the protocols, in a great many languages, and innocent, duped people actually believe this drivel.

A friend once showed me a photograph he had taken of a newsstand in Buenos Aires, where the Spanish-language version of the forgery was prominently displayed. And who was selling the newspapers and magazines? An elderly Jew, his beard and yarmulke prominent, who—my friend explained—was a recent arrival in Argentina, and earned his living at the kiosk, although he could not himself read Spanish.

Throughout Jewish history there have been wild accusations against Jews. One of the most persistent, and one of the most disgusting, is the blood libel—an accusation that used to surface prior to Easter (and Passover) in which Jews were charged with kidnapping a Christian child, to obtain fresh blood needed for the baking of Passover matza! As insane as the libel sounds today, there were Jews attacked and killed because of it.

In upstate New York, in the small city of Massena, early in the twentieth century, a small Christian child failed to return home from school. Like wildfire, the accusation spread against the tiny Jewish community—the Jews had killed the child, drained the blood, and would use it for Passover. Nobody knows what might have happened, but luckily the child showed up, fine and unharmed, and the blood libel evaporated.

Every now and then charges of international Jewry secretly owning all the banks in the United States crop up. One of the former chairmen of the U.S. Joint Chiefs of Staff, General Brown, sometime in the '70s was quoted as saying that Jews owned all the media, and manipulated it to help Israel. To which an elderly, poor Jew living in a modest Brooklyn apartment responded, "Nu, I wish it were true—we should all own the banks and be so rich!"

Actually, there does exist a worldwide Jewish network, but it's not a cabal nor a conspiracy. It's merely an extension of the strong sense of family that Jews have. When I travel in the United States or in Europe, I seek out a kosher restaurant. I have had the same experience in London, Paris, Antwerp, Houston, Los Angeles and Chicago—dining in a kosher restaurant is almost like eating at home; you look about you, and realize that your fellow diners could pass for your extended family. (In Israel, virtually the whole country gives you that reaction).

Charges of an international cabal amuse me. There was a story in the Jewish media recently from, of all places, Katmandu, Nepal, high up in the Himalayas. I wonder if that would be regarded as an international conspiracy.

Apparently Nepal has become a popular place for young Israelis to visit, especially those who have just completed their obligatory army service, and who feel they need a little time of respite between military life and the next phase of their lives, either a job or entering college. Nepal is also not expensive, and certainly a fascinating place to spend time in. Last Passover, the Israeli embassy in the Nepalese capital, realizing that there were apparently many hundreds of young Israelis visiting, as well as several dozen Jews from England and the United States, announced that a Passover seder would be held under a tent on the grounds of the embassy. Everyone was invited.

The Lubavich Hasidic movement, known for its outreach programs around the world, flew in two rabbis, hundreds of copies of the Passover Haggadah manual, and ample quantities of matza, wine and chicken. (Nepal is a vegetarian country). Some 800 people showed up for the seder, visitors from Israel, the United States, England and other places, and under the tent they sang and celebrated this oldest Jewish holiday, commemorating the exodus of the Israelites from Egypt more than 3,000 years ago.

Would the anti-Semites consider this an international conspiracy?

I remember once serving on a jury. We were twelve people, and only one other juror besides me was Jewish. It was important for us because the deliberations had been dragging on for several days, and now it was already close to noon and the two of us knew that Yom Kippur eve, the most sacred part of the Jewish year, would begin in a few hours. We had to go home, clean up, eat a big meal before the all-day Yom Kippur fast, and the minutes kept ticking away.

At about two in the afternoon, I finally knocked on the jury room door, which was promptly opened by the uniformed officer of the court, a tallish man.

"Pardon me," I began, "I wonder if you could ask the judge to dismiss my friend and me early—you see, we have to be home very soon to begin observance of the holiest day of the Jewish calendar. It's the beginning of Yom Kippur. I'm sure you've heard of it."

The officer smiled. "Relax, I already spoke to the judge and he'll send in word that you can both leave early. You see, I'm a *landsman,* and I also have to leave early."

Does the word *landsman* have a secret meaning? Nonsense. It's a Yiddish term that simply means someone who comes from the old country (land), and is used to refer to a fellow Jew.

A number of years ago, when the international popular show, "Fiddler on the Roof," was playing in several countries simultaneously, an incident took place in Texas that indicates how deeply most Jews value their Jewish identity. The smash Broadway play had been playing in Texas for several weeks, featuring nationally-known stars, when someone realized that the play was slated to appear on Yom Kippur eve, when the hallowed Kol Nidre prayer is recited once a year in thousands of synagogues around the world.

Leaders of the Jewish community approached the producer and asked that the play either close that evening, or at the least that the star—himself a Jew, who portrayed Tevya the milkman—be replaced. They said that for this Jewish performer to appear on Kol Nidre night would be unseemly. The star interrupted the discussions. He insisted he would appear, Yom Kippur or not.

That Texas Jewish community virtually boycotted the show after that; the story of the star's action made the wires and was picked up in the general and Jewish media. Jews throughout the country were shocked and embarrassed by his behavior, and there followed an unspoken decision not to attend any other shows he ever performed in. Sadly, it was the beginning of his professional decline. Jewish identity and Jewish self-esteem are qualities that most Jews, and probably most Gentiles, value highly. Flaunting a performance on the holiest night of the year, in the face of community requests to abstain, and in a show that the whole world admired and knew as a Jewish show, turned out to be a tragic error.

Most Jews probably never consciously think of their Jewish identity. They accept their Judaism as a norm, some more enthusiastically than others but it is generally not a subject they talk about too often.

That however is not true of college-age students, who spend at the least four years studying, analyzing, debating, and seeking answers, sometimes to difficult philosophical questions that have troubled mankind through the ages. I am thinking of one such college student; a Jew by birth, he nevertheless was denied any kind of religious or cultural education. In short, he knew nothing at all about Judaism. As luck would have it, his best friends in college were all Jewish, and all had had extensive Jewish educational experiences. All of them had also visited Israel.

So, one day this young man—very bright, very serious—decided that he too wished to visit Israel. He joined up with one of the many groups that spend an intensive three weeks in the country. They toured the old and the new, heard talks about the country's difficult political problems, met with Israelis their own age (and could not quite get used to seeing young women soldiers carrying their weapon with them). Like many other tourists, our visitor was deeply impressed with Jerusalem, which he called "the jewel of the country."

I asked him if he visited the Yad Vashem Holocaust Memorial. He grew serious, and chose his words carefully. "Yes, I did," he said. "It had a deep impact on me. Especially the children's pavilion." And then he added: "You know, I'm going to graduate school soon but I've also made up my mind to do a lot of physical training. You see, we Jews are very vulnerable."

The Yad Vashem Memorial had apparently left its mark on him. And this was probably the first time in his life, he is in his early 20s, that he had uttered the words "we Jews."

Paul Newman, the popular actor who is especially endeared to Jews for his role in the movie "Exodus," in which he stars as Ari Ben Canaan, the hero of the film, had a Jewish father and a Christian mother. He was once asked by an interviewer whether he considered himself Jewish or Christian, and he shot back a quick reply, his blue eyes twinkling, "Jewish."

How come? the interviewer persisted.

"It's more interesting," Newman said.

Perhaps so, after all we go back some 4,000 years; we have produced some of the greatest minds of the ages. A half-century ago fully one-third of our people was deliberately massacred while the world stood by idly. When you visit Israel, where it seems life is lived in a fast lane, and where one often gets the feeling that this was what it was like when the American settlers went west and were confronted by dangerous situations virtually on a daily basis, you look about you and wonder which of the older people went through the hell of a Nazi death camp.

Sometimes, when the weather is warm, one can see the tattoos on their arms. And sometimes, there is a certain ineradicable expression in their eyes that reveals their background. To say that all the Jews in Israel feel themselves to be members of one giant family is obvious. A young Israeli soldier killed in a terrorist action is mourned by the whole country.

Almost every Israeli Jew one meets has a poignant story to tell. Some stay with you forever.

I met a family in Tel Aviv that had come from Poland—a husband, wife and two daughters, one about 12 and the other 15. They had been allowed to emigrate to Israel in 1968 when there was a relaxation of the rules; about three-quarters of the Jews in Poland decided to leave.

The mother was Jewish and therefore so were the two

daughters. The husband was not. She told me the story, a few bits at a time.

When World War II broke out, following the Germans' invasion of Poland, she was about 16. Her parents feared for her safety and sent her to the country to live on a farm, whose owners they had known for a number of years. The farm was isolated, she could pass for a Gentile, and during the war years she worked on the farm, helped the farm family's son, a youth of 18, with his neglected school work, and when the war ended she rushed back to Warsaw to find out what had happened to her parents and sister and extended family. They had all been killed.

The young farmer with whom she had worked side by side for several years had accompanied her to the Polish capital. He now urged her to return home with him, explaining that she was alone in the world. He added that he loved her and wished to marry her, saying her being Jewish did not bother him. She could remain Jewish, he said, it would not interfere in their lives, and if there were children, they too could be raised as Jews.

What he did not add was that he had saved her life during the war years on a number of occasions when German patrols showed up unexpectedly. He had hidden her in a secret room behind the barn. She always felt she owed him her life.

They were married, and after a while the depression that had seized her after she learned of her family's total destruction left her. The husband's parents treated her like a daughter, and out of gratitude she often accompanied them to church, with her husband, so as not to embarrass them in front of the neighbors.

The two children came along after a few years, and the farm became a happy place. Although there were anti-Semitic outbreaks in postwar Poland, and the Communist government made sharp attacks against Jews, their isolated farm remained untouched. Until 1968, when the Jews of Poland were invited to leave.

She persuaded her husband that they would all be happier in Israel, and assured him he would find work as a tailor, a vocation he had learned, in addition to farming. They proceeded to Israel, were helped with an apartment in Tel Aviv, the girls entered school, and the husband turned part of their apartment into a small tailoring shop. They had been in Israel for about two years when I met them.

He was friendly enough, but we could not communicate— I don't know Polish, and he did not speak Hebrew or Yiddish. I could see that the girls were ebullient; they had mastered Hebrew, were excelling in school, and they seemed very happy. The mother worked as a saleslady, and sometimes found work as a Polish translator.

She told me when I went to pick up a jacket that her husband had done some work on that they were returning to Poland. I was astounded, and asked why. Speaking in Hebrew, she explained: My husband cannot find a place for himself here. He cannot learn Hebrew, he has almost no Polish Catholic friends, he feels he does not belong in Israel. He said to me, you and the girls can stay here—I see you are very happy. I will go back to the farm. Of course, I would prefer you come back with me, but I will understand if you choose to stay.

"I thought and I thought," she said. "He is such a good man. The father of my daughters. He saved my life. I cannot abandon him now." The tears had welled up in her eyes.

I have often wondered about that family. Did they remain in Poland? Will the daughters return to Israel now that they have had a taste of life in a Jewish majority? I never heard anymore.

There is a strong Jewish tradition that all Jews are responsible one for another. The tradition goes back many centuries. Historians note that in the Middle Ages, when virtually all travel was by sea, Jews would go out into the world to buy or sell merchandise and some of them would be subject to kidnapping by pirates. The pirates, it seems, had discovered that a Jewish captive could always be ransomed, and usually for a goodly sum. Thus a Jewish visitor from Venice who was on his way to Spain stood a good chance of being kidnapped, and the kidnappers might well ask for a ransom for him from his home community in Venice, as well as from his destination community.

The tradition of Jewish communities and individuals helping each other in perilous times has never died down. The percentage of funds raised by American Jews, for example, for the rescue of coreligionists in Russia, Arab states and other places is far above average. There is a feeling among Jews that every Jewish man, woman and child, anywhere in the world, is a precious member of a relatively small community, and therefore everything possible must be done to rescue that person from danger.

One of the most memorable stories demonstrating the principle of one Jew caring for another goes back to 1919, the year after the end of World War I, when much of Poland was gripped in icy winter weather, and the whole country was in need of food, fuel, clothes and virtually everything else. An orphaned Jewish man, in his mid-twenties, lived in a small hamlet, jobless, almost without food, and nearly hopeless. He sat one day in his small wooden shack, and saw that his coal supply was nearly depleted, and the only food that remained in the pantry was a sardine can. He paced the shack, a blanket draped around his worn clothes, wondering what he was going to do to survive the winter, and how he would provide for himself after spring arrived.

His gnawing hunger finally got the better of him, and he approached the sardine can, noticing that it had been wrapped in a months-old New York newspaper, the Jewish *Daily Forward*. He glanced at the paper idly, recalling that the sardine can had been part of a parcel of food that had been sent to him by the Joint Distribution Committee, the worldwide Jewish relief agency. Curious, he opened the Yiddish paper, turned a page and noticed an ad for warm, Long John-type underwear, known in Yiddish as *gotkes*. He stared at the ad hard, reading that the store where it was being sold seemed to be prospering, for they advertised a score of other clothing items.

But it was the *gotkes* that had caught the man's eye. If the store owner could send him a pair, he thought, he could keep warm in this miserable winter, and look for work. Otherwise he found himself cold and unable to think clearly. On an impulse he sat down and wrote a letter to the store owner. "I am a poor Jewish man, aged 25, alone in the world," he wrote in Yiddish. "I saw your ad for *gotkes* and I decided to write and ask if you could send me a pair as a gift, and when I will be able to, I will send you the money. I am constantly freezing here—please help me." He rushed to the village postmaster, and shipped the letter off, hopeful for the first time in many weeks.

A month later a package arrived for the young man. It was from America, and when he tore it open he found two pairs of Long Johns and a note. The letter said, "My dear friend, my heart goes out to you—here are two pair of *gotkes*. Don't worry about payment. I hope you prosper in the future." The recipient donned the first pair and felt warm immediately. He examined the second pair, and there in the breast pocket he found an American bill for $100. Such a sum at that time in postwar Poland was like diamonds falling from the sky.

Now warm and deeply grateful, the young man dashed off a letter of thanks and sent it to his benefactor. Within a few weeks, his situation had improved dramatically. With the $100 he was able to buy a small shop and sell groceries in the hamlet. Within a few years life in Poland had improved and the tiny shop was now a much bigger store, there was never a shortage of food or fuel in his shack, and he had even met and married a young lady from a neighboring village and with the help of her dowry they bought a small house.

Meanwhile, the two men exchanged greeting cards at least twice a year, on the eve of Rosh Hashanah and on the eve of Passover. Within a few years the Polish Jew sent payment for the Long Johns. The two men began to exchange photographs of their families—the New Yorker had four sons, and the Polish Jew had a son and a daughter. Quite suddenly, both men realized that they had been corresponding for ten years and had never even met each other.

In November of 1929, almost exactly a decade from the time they had first exchanged letters, a cablegram arrived in Poland from New York. It said: "Dear friend, desperately need financial help owing to crash. Please send whatever you can." The very same evening the Polish Jew entered the synagogue, where congregants were at their daily service. He spoke to them with deep emotion, explaining how his American friend had rescued him, and urging that they now all unite to aid this unknown coreligionist. Within a few hours some $500 had been collected, and that very night the sum was cabled to New York.

A letter of thanks arrived a few weeks later. The letter talked about a "crash" and people losing their businesses and livelihoods, and expressed gratitude for helping him save his store so that he could continue to provide for his family. The years passed, and now both men seemed to be financially stable, but the New Yorker, starting in the mid-1930s, began to write a different kind of letter to his Polish friend. His letters now strongly urged his friend to pack up his goods, take his family and leave at once for Palestine. "I feel in my bones that a terrible disaster will soon befall our brothers and sisters in Europe because of this madman, Hitler," the New Yorker wrote. "Please do not hesitate, but go while there is still time."

In 1937 the Polish family, now a husband and wife and three children, made their way to the Italian port of Trieste, and then by sea to Haifa. The friends' correspondence continued all through the war years, and the American friend was happy to read that his friend's family had adjusted well and were not in need of any financial support.

Finally, in the year 1952, the two men and their families met in Tel Aviv. It was obviously a very emotional meeting.

Neither ever thought that what they had done was unique. "Jews help each other," they said. "That's the way it is."

Why do Jews gravitate to certain neighborhoods and areas and not to others? Is it because they are clannish, as some anti-Semites have charged? No, but subconsciously most Jews—even Jews whose roots in the United States go back three or more generations—feel more comfortable among themselves. Put it another way: most Jewish parents are concerned that their children should marry a fellow Jew, and obviously living in a "Jewish" neighborhood will enhance that possibility. What's more the more Jewish a neighborhood, the less chance there is that there will be anti-Semitic outbreaks or graffiti or any form of hooliganism. Also, the more Jews in a particular area the easier it will be to establish and support a synagogue, a Jewish community center, religious schools, a kosher butcher shop, and the like. Some may call this clannishness, but Jews shrug the designation off. It just seems safer and more comfortable.

On my way back to New York one summer from a business trip to Israel my El Al airliner had to make an unscheduled stop in Iceland to take on more fuel (this was before jet engines became pervasive). It was August and although it had been in the 90s in Tel Aviv, the temperature in the Reykjavik airport must have been around 30 or 40. All of us on the flight remained indoors while the plane was being fueled.

I was studying a showcase of handmade Eskimo-type souvenirs when a young American soldier approached me, somewhat surreptitiously. (The U.S. Air Force maintains a big base there). When he spoke, I thought he had an accent that marked him as someone from Tennessee or Kentucky. He couldn't have been more than nineteen. He called my attention to the El Al plane, visible through the large window. The Star of David and the Hebrew lettering were unmistakable.

"You just get off that plane?" he asked, his voice low, He seemed to be looking to the right and left, almost stealthily.

"Yes," I said, now a little apprehensive.

"Can you tell me—when does Yom Kippur fall this year?" he asked.

I smiled, he smiled, I told him the date (he remembered it was early in the fall). At the time, he said, he was the only Jewish Air Force man on Iceland, and had no easy way of knowing when the major holidays took place. If I'd had a pocket calendar, a Jewish calendar, I'd have given it to him gladly.

That too is part of the alleged international Jewish conspiracy.

Chapter IV

In Quest of One's Jewish Identity

PROFESSOR MICHAEL A. MEYER, A LEADING HISTORIAN WHO teaches at Hebrew Union College in Cincinnati, said recently that American Jews understood their identity as a reflection of three major historical phenomena of the past few centuries—the Enlightenment, Anti-Semitism, and Israel.

Noting that only a tiny handful of Jews in the world are virtually "totally self-segregated," and impervious to outside influences, he explained, "nearly all contemporary Jews feel they are Jews and at the same time something not specifically Jewish as well. For some, Jewishness remains their principal orientation in life, the center of their being. These are mostly the serious religious Jews, of whatever specific denomination, who continue to believe in some sense of Jewish chosenness and special destiny.

"For others," Meyer continues, "enlightenment has drawn them almost entirely outside their Jewish identity. Reason and universalism have worn away their particular loyalty to Jews and Judaism. Some are basically universalists; others have substituted new particularisms for old. Most actively identifying modern Jews, however, have in one fashion or another absorbed the influence of enlightenment. They argue that their Jewishness has nothing to fear from science or widening cultural horizons and that their universal commitments do not interfere with their Jewish ones. To a greater or lesser extent they have succeeded in neutralizing the erosive influence that enlightenment exercised in the initial stages of modernization."

The fact of the matter is that for many decades Jews have been trying to understand what is meant by their Jewish identity. Most Jews will acknowledge that being Jewish is more than merely belonging to a group that adheres to the Jewish religion—but most of them will be hard put to explain exactly what they mean. Prior to the establishment of Israel in May 1948, the overwhelming majority of Jews in the world saw themselves as a people living among various nations. After Israel became a full-fledged nation, attitudes and perceptions changed. An American Jewish visitor to Israel viewing an Israeli army parade in Tel Aviv could not help but feel pride and joy that now, after so many centuries of bloodshed and homelessness, and powerlessness, Jews had reestablished their ancient nation. And, willy nilly, he was a member of that nation.

And then when he stood on Manhattan's Fifth Avenue and saw a U.S. army contingent go by on the Fourth of July or Veterans Day, he could not help but feel patriotic pride. Soon he realized he was a member of two nations, a realization that still takes some getting used to. The U.S. Supreme Court, by allowing Americans to be both American and Israeli citizens simultaneously, has made getting used to that sensation a lot easier.

Jewish identity never was a concept that was easy, cut and dried; explaining how one feels to oneself is difficult, explaining it to others looms much harder. It is also a concept that changes over the years. A relatively young American Jewish college student may very well have one conclusive concept in his mind of what his Jewish identity is, but by the time he has reached beyond the age of fifty, he may feel quite different. Meeting and knowing other Jews, raising one's children and wishing for them to retain the Jewish heritage and pass it on, perhaps brushing up against anti-Semitism, visiting Israel— all these factors may influence and alter his view of himself as a Jew. In many cases he may not realize, until he is somewhat along in years, how deeply imbedded in him is his Jewish identity.

Martin Buber, one of the greatest Jewish religious thinkers of the twentieth century, was once asked to explain precisely what is a Jew, perhaps even to produce a credo of Judaism or Jewishness. After a time he conceded that he could not. He explained that often Jews are something of a puzzle to themselves, while for Gentiles they produce anxiety because they are so difficult to classify. Their "otherness" has often been cited as one of the major reasons for pervasive anti-Semitism, while the Jews themselves often reacted bitterly to being shunted aside. When Shylock asked plaintively, "If you prick us, do we not bleed?" he reflected a genuine Jewish reaction to the world around us.

Another towering Jewish thinker of the twentieth century, Sigmund Freud, himself a secularist almost all his life, also could not come up with a reasonable definition of Jewish identity. He ignored the idea of faith, but at the same time he was not satisfied merely with Jewish ethnicity. In one of his famous talks before a Jewish audience he said that he admitted being irresistibly attracted by Judaism and by Jews. He attributed this pull to "an inner identity, the intimacy that comes from the same psychic structure."

In the month of May 1967, weeks before the outbreak of the Six Day War, a strange, powerful event took place in the American Jewish community. The news for weeks continued to announce that Egypt, Syria, Jordan and perhaps other Arab states were about to pounce on tiny Israel and drive her into the sea, putting an end to the barely twenty-year-old nation. Virtually without being solicited, Jews from all social strata, from all economic classes, those who prayed daily and those who had not been inside a synagogue in forty years, began streaming to the nearest synagogue, bringing funds to help in this crisis. The Jews feared that another Holocaust was in the making, and that the promised destruction of Israel would mean the total annihilation of Judaism and the Jewish people.

There were many moving stories: an elderly retired Jew living on a modest income brought the deed to his house, saying in effect, "Here, take it—what good to me is a house if Israel perishes?" In Hollywood, prominent actors, directors, producers and musicians arrived with vast sums of money; some of them had never even been known to be Jewish. A terrifying fear of Holocaust II enveloped nearly every Jew in the world, and many realized for the first time how strongly Jewish they felt within—something that they would have probably denied earlier had there been no threat to Israel.

When the Israelis launched their preemptive attacks early in June, and effectively won the war in six days, Jews throughout the world were both deeply grateful that a catastrophe had been averted, and proud to bursting that their coreligionists had learned so well to be modern-day Maccabees. The 1967 Six Day War was a turning point for Jews in all parts of the world. Israel's lightning victory gave every Jew outside the country a vicarious sense of heroism. All Jews, observers said, stood taller and prouder since that momentous time. Jewish identity had scored a major triumph.

In his seminal study on Jewish identity, "Jewish Identity in the Modern World," Professor Meyer observes that anti-Semitism continues to play a major role in determining Jewish identity. "Even in countries where anti-Semitism is least severe, like the United States," he writes, "Jews nonetheless believe they are potentially endangered. . . Supporting (Jewish defense organizations) serves as a means of Jewish identification in the present as it has in the past."

Noting that persecution of Jews in what used to be the Soviet Union, Syria, Ethiopia and other countries has "energized the Israeli sense of ethnic responsibility," Meyer contends that anti-Semitism "has become most important for Jewish identity . . . as the memory of the Holocaust. The intense consciousness of that event is felt as a particular imperative to preserve Jewishness and as a universal task—based on the Jews having been singled out—to prevent anything resembling a Holocaust in the future."

The distinguished British rabbi and scholar, Dr. Louis Jacobs, says that to be Jewish a Jew must believe in God, in Jewish peoplehood, and in the centrality of Israel in Jewish life. How people interpret these three precepts, how much emphasis is placed on each, these are challenges facing modern Jews. A Jew may go all through life not thinking too much about what is meant by the word "God," but chances are that if he or she should come face to face with a devastating illness, the helpful intervention of God in that situation will suddenly loom large.

Many modern Jews will say "I believe in God" but are really unable to explain what they mean. Most rabbis and Jewish religious teachers are ready to discuss the problem of defining God, or questioning His role in the world; Judaism does not teach blind, unquestioning faith. Quite the contrary, questioning and a bit of skepticism are often seen as healthy first steps toward a greater understanding of God.

Bill Moyers, the television host, once asked a rabbi—an Orthodox rabbi, who himself was a highly spiritual, almost ethereal individual—if it was true that some members of his congregation did not believe in God. The rabbi did not hesitate. Yes, he said, they told him that they enjoyed being Jewish, they enjoyed the religious service, the study programs, celebrating the holidays, feeling themselves part and parcel of the worldwide Jewish community. And then they added, "Some day, perhaps soon, we'll begin to understand what is meant by God, and then we'll believe."

But, among most Jews, the single factor that unites them most and that appeals to their innermost self the most is the concept of Jewish peoplehood. As Professor Meyer says: "Peoplehood . . . represents the strongest component of Jewish identity today . . . most religious Jews link Judaism closely to Jewishness. Their synagogue activities are ways of expressing ethnicity. Attending religious services is something Jews do as members of the Jewish people. . . Mostly, I trust, Jewishness will focus in the future, as in the past, on Zion. For Zion represents not only Jewish origins and Jewish unity; it is also the symbol of that Redemption which orients Jewish identity to its highest goal and gives it intrinsic meaning."

Intermarriage is by no means a new phenomenon; what's more there are many cases when Jews married to Gentile women who converted to Judaism are transformed into better, more religious Jews than if they had married Jewish women who were born into the faith.

Nearly two and a half thousand years ago, following the destruction of the first Holy Temple in Jerusalem, the major section of the Jewish population was living in Persia, where the benign King Cyrus ruled. One day, the king suggested to Ezra, a community leader, that he proceed to Judea, the ancient homeland, in order (as the Bible puts it) "to regulate Judaism and Jerusalem according to the law of God." Ezra was empowered to mete out punishment to those who violated the Torah laws.

When Ezra reached the Jewish homeland, he was shocked. Many Jews, especially from the wealthier classes, had married non-Jewish women and had begun to abandon Jewish customs and practices. Unafraid and uncompromising, Ezra with the assistance of loyal-to-Judaism local leaders dissolved the mixed marriages and expelled the non-Jewish wives and their children from the country.

A national assembly was convened and almost every Jew in the country was in attendance. Ezra read from a Torah scroll from dawn to noon; this went on for several days, after which all the assembled Jews pledged not to marry a non-Jewish woman. They also pledged to observe the Sabbath laws and to provide funds for the newly-constructed second Temple. In Jewish tradition, Ezra the Scribe is regarded as having saved Judaism from extinction. One Talmudic comment says that Ezra was worthy to receive the Torah from God, had Moses not preceded him.

In the 1990s no one is suggesting that intermarriages be dissolved by force, and that the Gentile partners be sent away. The solution to the intermarriage problem is being resolved, when it is resolved, in two ways: Prior to the marriage, the would-be bride or groom is generally urged to consider conversion to Judaism; if these arguments fail, and a couple intermarries, hope is always expressed that at some point in the future the non-Jewish partner in the union will decide to become a formal member of the Jewish community through conversion.

In World War II, one of the most courageous groups fighting against the Nazis were the partisans in Yugoslavia, led by Tito. The Germans were never really able to conquer them, despite many attempts to do so. A substantial number of the partisans were Jews.

When the war ended in 1945, the partisans dispersed and went home. The Jews, in all too many cases, discovered that their wives and children had been brutally killed during the war years. A group of the Yugoslav Jewish partisans decided, almost simultaneously, to begin their lives anew in the newly-proclaimed state of Israel. Most of them, before they left for Israel, married local Yugoslav Christian women, whose husbands or fathers had been killed by the Nazis. When they arrived in Israel, the partisans and their wives agreed to a rabbinical suggestion that they be converted en masse.

I visited this group about two years after they had arrived. They lived on a moshav, a farming settlement where they worked cooperatively. It was impossible not to notice the blonde women, the wives of the farmers, with Slavic features, wearing rather large Stars of David hanging from gold chains, speaking elementary Hebrew. All in all they seemed very happy. One of the husbands pulled me aside as I was making notes and said, "Write that they are better Jews than we are! On Shabbat (Sabbath), no work. On the holidays, we have celebrations. You won't find a single pig on this place. The women we brought here made us good Jews!"

One of the historic sidelights of Jewish history was Napoleon's convening of the ancient Sanhedrin, a parliamentary-type body that met in Paris in 1807. Questions were put to the 71 delegates in attendance: May Jews marry more than one wife at a time? (No). Do Jews regard fellow Frenchmen favorably? (Yes). Would Jews fight alongside fellow French Christians in the event of need? (Yes). Do Jews permit a Jew and a Christian to marry? The Sanhedrin delegates responded negatively, explaining that French law permitted it but Jewish religious law forbade it.

Two hundred years since that response, Jews living in France, the United States, England and other democratic countries have maintained that same position. It is against Jewish religious law for a Jew to marry outside his faith. And in addition to the ancient religious ban, there is another reason that is perhaps all the more poignant in the era that follows the Holocaust period: The number of Jews in the world is so small that every intermarriage constitutes a threat to the well-being and continuity of the Jewish people.

I remember attending a wedding in which the groom was a born Jew and the bride a former Catholic girl who had converted to Judaism. It was a lovely, lively affair, everyone was happy and having a good time—except the parents of the bride. After a while the father explained to me that he and his wife could not be reconciled to the daughter's abandoning the family's Catholic faith. In effect, he said, why doesn't the groom become a Catholic?

I tried to explain the numbers of Jews who perished during the 1933–1945 period when the Nazis ruled, and added, "we are so few—we simply can't afford to lose more through intermarriage." Unfortunately, he was not persuaded. The young couple now, a number of years later, have a happy marriage;

relations between the parents however can only be described as cool.

It is very difficult, perhaps even impossible, for a Christian to understand the pain that a Jew feels when he encounters open, raw anti-Semitism. The neo-Nazis who insist on their right to parade in front of synagogues or Holocaust memorials are opposed tooth and nail by individual Jews and by Jewish organizations. The same is true of militant anti-Semites found in the Black community.

Among themselves, however, Jews frequently wonder: Why don't the Christians fight these punks too? Why do you never see the American Legion confronting these Nazi punks? Didn't thousands of Americans die in the war against the German Nazis, and Italian and Japanese fascists? And what has happened to the hundreds of thousands of Blacks who were helped for many decades by individual Jews and by Jewish groups—why don't they take a stand against Black anti-Semitism?

These questions deeply trouble American Jews and impact on their concept of themselves. Their Jewish identity is shaped by many factors—by the home they came from, by parental attitudes towards Judaism and Jewishness, by personal experiences with fellow students in college, by encounters with Gentile co-workers, by their own knowledge of Judaism, or lack of it, and by the overall ambience vis-a-vis Jews in the country.

Certain events stand out. Peter Stuyvesant, when confronted with a total of 23 Jewish refugees who sought a haven in New Amsterdam, wished to expel them all. What saved them was "connections." Several members of the board of the Dutch company that was most influential at the time stopped him. In the Civil War, when circumstances were such that there were Jews fighting on both sides of the war, one of Lincoln's top generals, Ulysses S. Grant, found it fit to order the deportation of all Jews from Tennessee on false charges of profiteering. (Lincoln rescinded the order).

Before World War II, a virulently anti-Semitic priest in Michigan, Father Coughlin, had a radio audience of millions who listened to his pro-Hitler, anti-Semitic attacks every Sunday. It was only the Japanese attack on Pearl Harbor that put an end to his broadcasts. And just before we entered the war, we turned away a shipload of nearly 1,000 Jewish refugees, forcing the German captain to return to Europe, where most of the Jews perished in the Holocaust. The *Spirit of St. Louis* tragedy still haunts America's Jews.

These are the bits and pieces of collective Jewish memory that shape one's Jewish identity. Thus, when a son or daughter goes off to college and in the course of time brings home a young woman, or a young man, for the family to meet—is there any wonder that parents wonder? Who is this person that professes love for my child? Who are the parents, the siblings? How can I feel assured that there is no anti-Semitism in that family? Even if I feel myself compelled to agree to my child's wish to intermarry, and even if I can only hope that one day in the future this intermarriage will lead to a conversion to Judaism on the part of the non-Jew—how can I be absolutely sure that this is not a family where hatred for Jews is as natural as flowers in the spring?

One of the great justices of the U.S. Supreme Court was Louis D. Brandeis. And yet his nomination by President Wilson was opposed by many senators and approval of his nomination was very close. Then, after a few years, Brandeis noticed a strange situation within the chambers of the court. One of his fellow justices did not speak to him. He did not say good morning, or smile, or nod. He simply acted as though Brandeis was not there. Brandeis was puzzled and asked another justice on the court to make inquiries. Sheepishly and shamefacedly the judge explained to Brandeis: "He said he does not talk to Jews."

Jewish identity in America is therefore a tricky business. Is it possible that some Jews, men and women, subconsciously believe that if they marry a Gentile they will automatically be accepted by the overwhelming majority and therefore need never again be concerned with anti-Semitism? Probably. These are deliberate, conscious assimiltationists who set out to

change their names in the hope that their minority status will
be transformed at once to majority.

To me these people, fortunately few in numbers, are pa-
thetic, even tragic. Do they really believe that they will succeed in disappearing into the mainstream? Can one imagine
how they must tremble every time someone talks of Jews, or a
Jewish issue, or Israel, or tells an anti-Semitic joke?

I went to school with a neighbor's son named Jacob Mar-
kowitz. Our paths went in very diverse directions. One day,
after more than forty years, we bumped into each other in a
hotel lobby. I was genuinely happy to see him. "Jake!" I said,
pumping his hand. He seemed to pale, looked about him
nervously, and then whispered, "No, I've changed my name—
I've been John Moore for quite a while."

He certainly was not true to his own self. He looked pros-
perous enough but also unrelaxed, nervous, anxious to get
away. We said our goodbyes, and I let him go, back to his life
that must be filled with deceptions—mostly to himself.

The only rabbis in the United States who perform intermarriages are Reform rabbis. Approximately 50 per cent of these
rabbis do so, not always but occasionally. (A small number do
so together with Christian clergymen). These rabbis have a rationale: By officiating at an intermarriage, they insist, they
will hopefully influence the non-Jewish partner in the union to
decide at some future date to convert and become Jewish. The
other explanation is far more pragmatic. Members of a Reform
Temple for many years who are forced to give their consent to
a child's intermarriage feel they need their rabbi's moral support in such a difficult moment, and probably most Reform
rabbis would agree.

I attended one such wedding not so long ago. Both partners
in the marriage were physicians. The groom was Jewish, the
bride Christian. Half of the wedding party were Jews, and half
were Christians. There was an unmistakable coolness between
both groups. In the traditional wedding ceremony, the groom
says to his bride as he places the wedding band on her finger:
"You are consecrated unto me with this ring according to the

laws of Moses and Israel." In this intermarriage the rabbi changed the last few words to say, "according to the laws of God." The Jewishness of the ceremony seemed to evaporate right there.

Nowadays, by and large, Jews do not proselytize. It is against Jewish tradition to go out and actively seek converts; oddly enough, however, this was not always so. In the first and third centuries, for example, the Talmud records active Jewish conversion efforts, with one rabbi explaining that Jews were brought into the world to seek out non-Jews and convince them of the beauty and joyfulness of Judaism.

The first-century Jewish historian, Josephus, records that in his time more women than men opted to become Jewish. Possibly the men of the time feared the need to undergo circumcision.

After the Roman empire collapsed and was succeeded in much of Europe by Christianity it became a capital offense to convert to Judaism. From that time on, conversions dwindled and virtually ceased. By the end of the Middle Ages, the Jewish communities began to discourage any would-be converts, for now they feared that if a Christian chose to become a Jew, the Jewish community involved would also suffer.

There have been in modern times many Christian converts to Judaism who have become active, exemplary members of the Jewish community, in the United States, in Israel, and in other countries. One such convert was a former Catholic priest who eventually became a much-beloved teacher of Talmud in a Brooklyn yeshiva. One woman convert, Rachel Cowan, has become a Reform rabbi. Another woman convert in California divorced her Jewish husband on grounds that he was not a religious enough Jew.

Chapter V

Only Jews Can Feel Pain of Anti-Semitism

THE DISTINGUISHED HISTORIAN, LUCY DAVIDOWICZ, IN HER book *On Equal Terms,* a summation of Jewish life in America from 1881 to 1981, noted that after the Six Day War in 1967, and more than a generation after the impact of the Holocaust had begun to fade on the conscience of the world, a new wave of anti-Semitism swept over the earth. Swastikas were scrawled on synagogues, Jewish institutions and Jewish cemeteries in western and eastern Europe, and in the United States.

As though it was a reaction to Israel's swift and almost miraculous victory, Poland, for example, between June 1967 and 1970 drove the Jews "from all government and (Communist)

party posts, and ended by driving them from the party itself."
Jews in all sections of the world who had begun to believe that
they could integrate peacefully into the lives of the nations
among whom they lived were brutally shocked into a sharp
awareness—the sick phobia called anti-Semitism does not
seem to die, it merely goes into hibernation, lies quietly for
years, even decades at a time, and then erupts with the sudden
swiftness and power of a tornado.

The Jews in the (then) Soviet Union numbering in the millions, who had been forcibly cut off from all contact with Judaism, Zionism, Hebrew, Jewishness and Jewish communities
abroad, and who had come to believe that they could intermarry and live peacefully among fellow Soviets, and gradually
disappear as Jews, were rudely, painfully awakened. No matter
how long they lived in the Soviet Union, no matter how
deeply they were committed to the country, no matter how
hard they worked for the advancement of the country, when all
was said and done, they were still Jews.

In the face of a clear-cut threat to Israel's existence, in the
months preceding June 1967, the anti-Semites of the world,
led by the Soviets and the Arabs, and aided to a lesser extent
by the west, unashamedly designated Israel an aggressor state
and condemned it in the most vicious terms. The reaction of
the Jews in the Soviet Union and her satellites—in spite of a
controlled press and radio and television that aired lies on top
of lies about Israel and Jews in general—was an historic turn-
around in which a decades-old belief in Socialism as the wave
of the future was discarded, and fearlessly Jews in that hapless
part of the world began to proclaim a return to their roots.

Almost no one had predicted such a development, although
earlier visits by Elie Wiesel and the Israeli activist Aryeh Eliav
had called attention to the Soviet Jews' silent but ardent desire
to re-affiliate with the Jewish people. It was as though a prodi-
gal son had strayed far from his roots and then spun around,
embraced his parents and tearfully said, "I'm coming home!"

The Jewish identity that the overwhelming majority of the
Soviet Jews had shed in the wake of the Bolshevik revolution—when atheism became the law of the land, when Juda-

ism was outlawed as a bourgeois faith and culture—this same Jewish identity was suddenly and proudly adopted by the Russian Jews. The Six Day War that Israel had won had succeeded not only in saving the Jewish state from a Holocaust, but it had also made every Jew in the world take renewed pride in being Jewish; in the Soviet Union, the Jews' long-suppressed Jewish identity had struggled through the decades-old layers of anti-Semitism, enabling the Soviet Jews to assert and feel that they too had again become part of the Jewish people. It was one of the great, historic moments in Jewish history.

In the free and democratic United States, quite another phenomenon took place on the heels of the Six Day War. In Jewish history, anti-Semitism had always stemmed from the extreme right, but the Soviets' vitrolic anti-Israel stance was followed by an anti-Semitism in the United States that emanated from the New Left, which soon found common ground with the Third World, and with Communist China and Cuba, and with Black extremists. Thus, the anti-Semitism from the Black community shocked American Jews. They were inured to bigotry and threats from fascist and Nazi elements, but the open hatred directed at them from the Blacks was unexpected and almost inexplicable. After all, Jews asked one another, who had been the Blacks' best friends and most devoted supporters if not the Jews? And this is how we're rewarded? they asked.

Sociologists explained the new phenomenon by linking the young Blacks' anti-Vietnam stance, and the whole youth cultural uprising and the widespread use of drugs, but for most Jews the explanations were not enough. They remained, and to a large extent still remain, unable to accept the hostility directed at them from the Black community.

These developments impacted sharply on Jews and their concept of themselves. Most Jews seemed to find strength within their own community. More and more Jews began to immerse themselves in Jewish studies, in greater observance of religious rituals, in a feeling that only fellow Jews really cared about their future welfare. More young adult Jews began to

wear their yarmulkes in public, and could be seen among doctors in hospitals, lawyers in court, and teachers on campus.
One such young college student who always sported a yarmulke, and who was known not to be observant of Jewish religious laws was asked why. His answer was typical of a new
attitude: "*Davka,* just because, that's why. I want them to
know I'm a Jew."

Dr. Norman Lamm, president of Yeshiva University, wrote
recently that although there are a growing number of young
American Jews who are being "turned on" to Judaism there is
also a "negative side—the past two decades have seen a dis-
tressing acceleration of the rate of assimilation and intermarriage, which threaten to unravel the fiber of American Jewish
life." One can say that the overwhelming majority of American Jews—those who are Orthodox, Conservative, Reform,
Reconstructionist or secular—share Dr. Lamm's distress with
the accelerating number of Jews who marry non-Jews and
who, in the vast majority of cases, slip away from Judaism.
Very few Jews actually convert to Christianity, but the total effect is the same—to all intents and purposes, they cease being
Jewish and their children tend to join the mainstream religion, which of course is Christianity.

A recent issue of the official organ of the United Synagogue
of Conservative Judaism published a challenging headline to
its adult readers. It said: "Is it a foregone conclusion that to
send one's son or daughter to a secular university will consign
him/her to the threat of intermarriage, drug use or abuse,
AIDS, and so forth?"

The answer is quite forthcoming. Of the more than 2,500
colleges and universities in the United States, there are only
30 to 40 "campuses in the country that offer the kind of Jewish
ambience and Jewish student body that will enable a student
with clear Jewish concerns and needs to feel comfortable." Although there are many Hillel centers catering to Jewish college students' needs, they are not all equal in quality and
impact. Parents are strongly advised to visit a Hillel center on

a Shabbat, and personally try to judge whether it is a suitable place for their child.

Thus, exposing a college-age student to a whole new world can be a risk for that student's sense of Jewish identity. How it will all turn out depends on the number of fellow Jewish students on campus, on the quality of Jewish studies programs available at that campus, on the wisdom of the local Jewish adviser who is called upon to respond to attacks on Jews and on Israel, and of course on the kind of Jewish home the student grew up in, prior to going off to college.

There is an odd situation in the American Jewish community that is tied directly to the problem of intermarriage. Jewish youngsters, from quite early years, usually attend a synagogue's religious school, starting first with nursery school, then entering the afternoon school (since the majority of children go to public school), and then by the time they get to Bar or Bat Mitzvah age, both they and their parents all too often feel they've had enough. The children drop out of religious school in their early teens, with rare exceptions; they cease attending religious services, as do their parents; the parents also suspend their memberships.

There are of course exceptions. There are families where religious services are a regular part of a family's life. There are teenagers who attend Jewish high school programs and continue to come to synagogue on a regular basis. But these are the exceptional situations. (The Orthodox children who study at all-day schools are also in a separate category. Their homes are strictly observant, and their lifestyle is far more geared to the synagogue than most other families, but they remain in the minority).

So, from roughly age thirteen to the middle or late twenties, a very large percentage of Jewish youths are out of touch with the synagogue, with Jewish study programs, with Judaism's fundamental requirement that a Jew continue to learn always, every day, throughout the year. Certainly there are many exceptions—most Jews arrange or attend a Passover seder, a great many return to synagogue on Rosh Hashanah and Yom Kippur (the High Holy Days), many recite the traditional *yahrzeit* memorial prayer for a parent or a loved relative on four holidays and also on the yearly anniversary of the individual's death. Many Jews remain active, or become active in one or more Jewish organizations. They thus receive at home various periodicals, most of which disseminate Jewish educational material.

Nevertheless, there remains a great hiatus in Jewish living and study for most youngsters roughly between the ages of thirteen and the age when they decide to get married. If the couple is Jewish, and the ceremony is conducted by a rabbi, that happy moment serves to bring the newlyweds a bit closer to Jewishness. Many synagogues offer newlyweds greatly reduced membership dues, in the hope that they will eventually become permanently affiliated, which is often the case.

In a very large number of cases, what happens after marriage involving a Jewish couple is that both partners at first concentrate on building the marriage, on their careers, on making new friends as a new couple, and only after a time do they think of joining a synagogue, especially after they have a child and they look about them and see that other young couples in their age category do the same thing. It is not surprising to see a young Jewish mother or father, aged approximately thirty, entering a synagogue, escorting a small child to a nursery class, meeting people their own age, developing friendships, and before long becoming more and more involved with the social, religious, educational and other programs of the synagogue.

Where the problems arise are with an intermarried couple.

It begins when the non-Jewish partner may balk at living in a so-called Jewish neighborhood. A compromise follows. The Jewish spouse brings his or her Christian spouse to the Jewish parents' home for a seder, or for the High Holy Day services, or for the annual Chanukah candle-lighting ceremony. For some Christians, these celebrations may be familiar, but for others they may be very foreign, and perhaps even bizarre.

Then there is the opposite side of the coin. The Christian partner brings the Jewish spouse into the family home. In some homes the crucifix may be prominently displayed, or some of the guests may be wearing crosses. Somewhere in the back of the Jew's mind there is a memory of something that was learned a long time ago—the Crusaders attacked and murdered thousands of Jews on their journeys to the Holy Land, all in the name of the cross, or a memory of someone noting that the Pope who sat in the Vatican during the years of World War II never once raised his voice against the Nazi massacres of the European Jews.

Perhaps there will be an awkward moment, unintentional but uncomfortable nevertheless, when someone at the table will pass a plate of food to the Jewish guest and say something like, "Do you people eat this?" With the best of intentions, of course, that particular individual knowing only that Jews refrain from certain foods and not really knowing which those banned dishes are.

The real painful problems begin, of course, in an intermarriage, when a child is born. If it is a boy, the Jewish partner may strongly wish to have the new-born son circumcised, a rite that is deeply-rooted in Judaism. There may be an objection from the Christian parent, that the ancient ceremony is "barbaric" and the Jewish partner may well respond that most people in America have their sons circumcised by a surgeon, for health reasons.

If the Jewish partner in this intermarriage is the father, and the son in question is a first-born there is an additional ceremony, the redemption of the first-born, that must also be observed. The Jewish father may explain to his non-Jewish wife, or he may not, depending on the particular situation, that a circumcision ceremony is a biblical command, in which the special covenant that exists between God and the Jewish people is being reaffirmed. The words from Genesis that he learned as a small child may come back to him: "Every male child among you shall be circumcised throughout the generations . . . and the uncircumcised male . . . shall be cut off from his people . . . he has broken My covenant."

While the intermarried couple may rejoice that a healthy male child was born to them, they certainly are not enjoying the disagreement that may ensue about the circumcision. The

Jewish parents may sense that not having a circumcision for the child would be a great sin, a clear-cut rejection of God's command; that parent may also have read of the thousands of Russian Jews who emigrated to the United States and Israel, and the many who immediately sought to be circumcised in order to feel full-fledged members of the Jewish community. For the Christian parent, the whole idea must in all likelihood seem abhorrent and atavistic. If the Jewish parent is the mother, she may desist from making too much of a fuss over this issue, for she may know—correctly—that the little boy, circumcised or not, is Jewish, since he is the child of a Jewish mother.

Of course, the Christian parent may wish to have the new-born child baptized, and again there may well be resistance from the other spouse. If the intermarried couple is wise and considerate, they will try hard to keep all these painful discussions between the husband and wife away from their parents, and other family members. Involving them can only cause more pain for more people.

Let us assume that a year or two go by. The young mother, who is the Christian partner, is wheeling her child down the street on a sunny day. She passes the synagogue and sees young mothers of her own age picking up their children from nursery school. What goes through her mind? She has heard that this particular school is very well-regarded; should she send her child there? All the other children are Jewish, the wall decorations have Jewish motifs, the youngsters will learn Jewish songs, and on Friday they will learn to bless the wine and the challah, and prepare for the Sabbath. Her husband, she muses, would undoubtedly be very happy, but could she do it? What about a Christian school? Would the child feel uncomfortable, knowing that he is half and half? And if the child came home clutching a cross, how would her husband feel? She remembers hearing from him once that in the old country, where his grandparents originated, the advent of Easter and Christmas was a time to attack Jews.

She is filled with misgivings, doubts, confusion. The best thing, she decides, is to raise the child, and any future children, without any religious affiliation at all. That way, when they are grown and adult, they can choose any faith—or no faith—they wish.

She continues to think. Wait, she has heard that a very large number of the young men and women who become ensnared by the cults come either from broken homes, or from homes where no religion whatsoever was observed. Do I want my child to grow up to become a Moonie, or a Hare Krishna, or one of those? Isn't a religious upbringing a strong underpinning for a child nowadays? As science expands, many old values seem to be declining; crime is rampant along with drugs. Wouldn't I be a very bad parent if I did not give my child all the support he needs so that he grows up to become a fine, upstanding, responsible person?

There are only two sure ways to prevent intermarriage and all the difficult problems and sometimes heart-wrenching pain it brings in its wake. One way is the Hasidic way, i.e., by and large Hasidic parents simply isolate their children from the rest of the world, including the Jewish community at large, and when the child is of age, a marriage with a suitable partner from a good family is arranged. And that's it.

A second way is to move to Israel, where the majority of the population is Jewish. Mathematically, the chances are excellent that a youngster will meet another Jewish youngster and they will marry and remain Jewish. There are exceptions in Israel, however. Sometimes a Gentile visitor or resident of Israel meets a Jewish Israeli, they fall in love and get married, and both sets of parents have to accept their decision.

But for most Jews living in the free, open society that characterizes the western democracies, the mathematical equations are such that Jews and Gentiles will meet, some will marry, a small number of the Gentiles will convert to Judaism, and most of the Jews in the intermarriages will allow themselves to simply be absorbed into the majority religion and culture. Yes, many of the Jewish partners will assure their parents that they "will raise the children as Jews" but pretty much everyone knows they are merely mouthing empty words.

In a recent article in an Israeli magazine, Lawrence M. Reisman, a lawyer, cautioned Jews against devoting too much time to secular studies. He says: "The non-ultra-Orthodox Jew may admire the acculturized Jewish societies of the past, but the reason he or she is Jewish today is because his or her ancestors were, by and large, not part of those societies." His solution for the battle against intermarriage is for Jews to remain separate and apart from the general culture. "The Jewish societies (of the Middle Ages) that produced poets, philosophers and scientists have disappeared, while those that produced close-minded Talmudists remained vitally Jewish. In the ancient world, the Hellenized Jews of Alexandria eventually assimilated; the separatist Jews of Palestine and Babylonia survived."

There are some plain-spoken American Jews who do not object to the total assimilation of the Jewish community. They believe sincerely that this will eliminate anti-Semitism once and for all; they also believe that the fight for Jews to continue to exist as Jews is simply too great. What they are saying in effect is that Jews have made extraordinary contributions to society for more than 4,000 years but it is now time for the Jewish people to simply give up its own identity, and become part of the nations among whom they live.

Fortunately, they remain a very small minority in the Jewish community. Most Jews maintain that we were and are a great people, and we hope to continue to be a "light unto the nations." Jews like to note with pride, for example, that although we are less than one percent of the world's population, the percentage of Nobel Laureates who are Jewish is around 30 percent. Of course, we have our share of criminals and wrong-doers, but we do have a disproportionately large share of scientists, artists, musicians, physicians, professors—people who contribute to society and do whatever they can to advance civilization.

In 1990 and 1991 a huge number of Soviet Jews emigrated to Israel, fleeing what they perceived as potential pogroms, and at the same time seeking to reestablish their long-suppressed Jewish identities. They numbered about a half-million people, more than ten percent of the existing Israeli Jewish population. (It is as though 25 million immigrants would arrive in the United States in a period of about fifteen months—all of whom would need jobs, homes, and intense language instruction).

Little Israel managed to provide homes for all, Hebrew instruction for all, and jobs in their fields for 60 percent of the immigrants—the other 40 percent preferred to remain unemployed until suitable jobs came along.

The Israelis who watched the television images of the newcomers arriving every day by air from various east European departure points could not fathom the facts that were presented—large numbers of the newcomers were doctors and scientists and musicians. Where, they wondered, are the plumbers, electricians and carpenters? Part of Jewish identity, it seems, includes being attracted to vocations that are people-oriented, and that have the promise of helping society, finding cures for diseases, making life easier for mankind.

Rabbi Adin Steinsaltz of Jerusalem, one of the great spiritual leaders of the twentieth century, suggests that there is so much laxity in young people today because essentially they are aimless. Judaism, he teaches, is a faith with a focus that enables a practitioner to set goals for himself and then attain them. For example, he explains, the exodus of the Israelite slaves from Egyptian bondage was a greater event than God's giving of the Torah to the freed slaves at Mount Sinai because it required the Israelites—who at the time were slaves in mind, body and spirit—to make a leap of faith, and believe that they would be led out of bondage, safely and successfully, and that they would reach a new home and a new life in the Promised Land. It was this spark of faith that enabled them to overcome all obstacles—and it is this same kind of spark of faith that can enable a Jew to believe that his life has a purpose and a goal, and that he can attain his goals. Rabbi Steinsaltz explains:

"The essence of the Exodus is in the initial, faith-motivated decision to leave the ordinary, the routine life, and to follow

God. This is that all-inclusive point of departure. Prior to that, there is nothing; all the rest is elaboration."

If a Jew living in modern times, in democratic America, believes that the Jewish heritage is worth preserving and passing on, and that the Jewish people have made extraordinary contributions to society, and will continue to do so, and that leading a Jewish life can be a happiness-producing lifestyle filled with intellectual challenges and ethical rewards, then it is incumbent on him/her to make superhuman efforts to marry a fellow Jew.

Intermarriage—where both partners remain members of their original, respective religions—is a sure step to a rocky, difficult road in life. When two young people of the same faith decide to marry, it is tough enough for them to get to know each other, to compromise with one another on important and insignificant issues, to grow together harmoniously and lovingly to be a role model for children. Marrying a spouse from another faith only adds additional problems.

What many young would-be marrieds do not realize until after the wedding ceremony is that when you wed your spouse, you are ipso facto also marrying his/her family. And also his/her many earlier years of schooling, religious practices, experiences, prejudices.

For every marriage partner, marriage is a preeminently difficult and crucial step. If the marriage is an intermarriage, in most cases each person is starting out with a severe handicap.

Chapter VI

Changing Religions Is a Very Big Step

DR. EGON MAYER, A LEADING SOCIOLOGIST WHO HAS WRITten extensively on intermarriage and who has led a number of surveys determined to throw light on the problem, wrote recently that "not more than two in 100 young Jews married Christians in America as late as in the 1920s. By the early 1980s nearly four out of ten did." By the 1990s, according to new studies, the intermarriage rate in the United States has surpassed 50 per cent, with some scholars claiming it is inching towards 60 per cent.

It is clear that there are Jewish families—assimilated, indifferent, apathetic to Judaism—who do not really care. Some of these families may even welcome an intermarriage, believing that it will close the gap between Jews and Christians and finally put an end to anti-Semitism. They often point to Hawaii, noting that there Polynesians, Japanese immigrants, Caucasians from the mainland and other racial minorities have all intermarried, producing new sub-groupings, without any difficulties.

One of the weaknesses of this argument, of course, is that these intermarrieds were all Christians, or were in the process of becoming Christians. Intermarriage between a Jew and a Christian is an entirely different matter—centuries of religious experience, traditions, and culture accompany the young couple to the bridal canopy. And much of this long history is not, unfortunately, pleasant and positive.

Dr. Mayer, in his surveys, has pointed out that the "rapid growth of intermarriage has created extraordinary family circumstances for hundreds of thousands of families—Jews and Christians alike. . . . Those who live in such marriages," he adds, "know that living with intermarriage generally does not generate any grand ideological conclusions. Rather, it constitutes an often delicate balancing between the pulls and tugs of love and tradition; a balancing between the loyalties to individuals and loyalties to ancestral memories; attachments to the compelling present and affinities to a lingering past.

"Parents of intermarrieds," Mayer continues, "are often hurt and puzzled by what they see in their children's marriage as a rejection of their own values and traditions. They frequently sense that they have failed somehow as parents in conveying the importance of their heritage to their children."

Rabbi Ephraim Buchwald, who is associated with New York's dynamic Lincoln Center Synagogue, eschews academic terminology and asserts that in the 1990s what is "killing America's Jews" is their obsession with the Holocaust. All Jews, he quickly explains, must continue to remember the catastrophe that overtook European Jewry during the brief period of Nazi hegemony. Nevertheless, he warns, while we must remember and of course never allow such a disaster to recur, obsessing with this event is leading to the demise of American Jewry.

This emphasis on the Holocaust, Buchwald maintains, has frightened American Jews. "Two million American Jews are now walking away from Judaism," he cautions. "They do not acknowledge that they are Jews." Further, he says, "one million American Jewish children are being raised as non-Jews or with no religion at all." No fewer than 625,000 American Jews, Rabbi Buchwald claims, "or their children have converted out of Judaism."

A Gallup poll recently said that while Catholics and Protestants both seem to be enjoying a renewal of interest in their faiths, in the Jewish community what is happening is that Jews are simply drifting away.

Buchwald attributes a number of reasons for this situation, which he describes as a "meltdown" rather than a melting pot. Jewish education, he charges, is inadequate, and when young Jews walk away from Judaism it is out of ignorance and not out of dissatisfaction with their ancient faith. As he puts it: "The ignorance is overwhelming—the average American Jew knows who was the mother of Jesus but doesn't have a clue as to who was the mother of Moses. He probably knows the meaning of the word 'trinity' but is unlikely to know what the word 'mitzvah' means. An American Jewish child can probably sing the first verse of 'Deck the halls with boughs of holly' but is unfamiliar with the first line of 'Ma'oz Tsur,' the joyous Chanukah hymn."

Why have the young Jews abandoned Judaism in such large numbers? One of the principal reasons many rabbis, including Rabbi Buchwald cite, is the wretched quality of most afternoon Jewish religious schools. Instead of providing a modicum of Jewish education for Jewish youngsters, these schools often turned off Jewish children.

Intermarriage and assimilation are inevitable in the present environment and these in turn will lead—in as few as 25 or 30 years—to a sharp diminution of the American Jewish community. The only logical way to stop the hemorrhaging of Jewish life in the United States is by concentrating all forces on intensive, joyous, positive educational programs for young and old.

The problem with the Holocaust memorials is that they focus on Jews as victims of Nazism. The emphasis should be instead on the joyousness of being a Jew, on the fulfillment that Jews derive from leading committed Jewish lives, and on disseminating song and dance, teaching and learning, joy and fulfillment—transforming the memory of the Holocaust into the chief focus of our lives as Jews scares younger generations away. Certainly we must remember what happened in the black years of 1933 to 1945, but students of Jewish history know that there have been other disasters, other massacres, other pogroms, and the reason we are still here, still functioning, is that we did not allow those horrific events to set the parameters of our lives as Jews. We mourned, we remember—and then we go on. Excessive remembering or mourning is counterproductive.

One of the Jewish people's most interesting and poignant innovations is the concept of the "ethical will," a last will and testimony that dates back to the early Middle Ages. In these final statements before death, a father would put down on paper the values he had learned in his lifetime, and that he hoped his children would profit from.

These ethical wills through the last centuries record the real ethical teachings that the writer had learned in his lifetime and that he considered important enough to transmit. Some of the most moving of these messages were actually composed in the last fifty years. A Jewish woman, Shulamit Rabinovich, trapped with her fellow Jews in the Nazis' ghetto in Kovno, begged her children in a message "to be just and honest—under normal circumstances this is so easy," she added. "Don't take foolish things to heart, and don't mourn for us with tears and words but rather with deeds."

One American synagogue asked its members, prior to the annual Yom Kippur fast day when Jews are expected to think about their ethical life in the year just gone by, and to plan for a better year in the new year, to write ethical wills.

One congregant, a physician, wrote: "More than materialistic possessions, I hope I will have left you . . . an optimistic spirit, a fervor and enthusaism for life, a closeness and regard for each other, and a sense of worthwhileness about yourselves."

These sentiments express beautifully Judaism's generally hopeful outlook on life and on the future. The irony of the American Jewish community in the final years of the twentieth century, indeed the tragedy, is that uninformed, uneducated Jews mistakenly believe that Judaism is a faith of sadness and sorrow, rather than a religion that celebrates life. Indeed the most precious element in all Jewish teaching and tradition is life—but tragically few Jews understand that.

More than one Gentile convert to Judaism, after a number of years of living as a Jew, has turned to the born Jew in the marriage and said, "You never told me it's so much fun to be Jewish!"

If a Jew decides to leave the Jewish community and convert to another religious faith, that is his right and his privilege. After all, we live in modern times and in a democratic society. I for one am very troubled whenever I learn of a Jewish young man or woman opting to bow out of Judaism and become a Christian, a Moslem or a member of any other religion. But—when I realize that the would-be convert out of Judaism knows nothing, absolutely nothing, about the faith into which he was born, then I become very aggravated. What a pity!

To change one's religious affiliation, to or from Judaism, is a deeply difficult thing to do; perhaps that is why converts to Judaism are generally welcomed with open arms, warmly, and every effort is made to make the new Jew feel comfortable and at ease, as though he or she has been a member of the Jewish community in good standing for a lifetime.

How traumatic it must be for a Jewish young man or woman who decides to give up being Jewish, and who really is totally ignorant of our faith, culture, philosophy, history, customs, practices and aspirations. To me, it is like a person marooned on an island who finds a treasure trove, but since he has no key and no idea of what's inside, he discards it, and it returns to the depths of the sea.

Most people know that both Christianity and Islam, the two religions most prevalent in the western world today, are in a very real sense offshoots of Judaism. In fact there was a time in the early years of the Roman empire, when the leaders of Rome—who had decided to put away their pagan idols and become monotheists—almost chose Judaism to become the state religion. It did not happen; Christianity was selected, and strict rules were promulgated forbidding anyone to convert to Judaism. (Islam did not appear on the scene until centuries later).

The best-selling American author Rabbi Harold Kushner, in a new book titled *To Life!* asks a hypothetical question of the reader: "How (or why) should you be Jewish?" and replies that Judaism is not the problem. "Life is the problem, and Judaism is the answer, and the question in the first place should have been "How can I be truly human?"

Rabbi Kushner continues: "You (the reader) may have come away from your childhood exposure to Jewish learning with the impression that Judaism was a collection of irrelevant customs and unconnected prohibitions stemming from its origins in ancient times."

How right he is! There are vast numbers of American Jewish adults who experienced that kind of education. Aged somewhere between eight and thirteen usually, they had to spend a few afternoons a week, after public school, in the synagogue's religious school, while their friends played ball outdoors, or took music lessons, or joined an after-hours school club devoted to astronomy or chess. These youngsters attended religious school because their parents and grandparents wanted them to, to master the Hebrew alphabet so that they could open a prayerbook and read the prayers, and so that they could read the biblical and prophetic portions on the Sabbath of their bar or bat mitzvah—and then enjoy a lavish reception where they would receive numerous gifts.

Did those youngsters learn the ethics of Judaism? Did they study the basic teachings and try to relate these concepts to their own lives, and to the world around them? Of course not. They were, firstly, very young; secondly, a teacher who was able to convey Jewish precepts to young children was a rarity; thirdly, the rabbi of the synagogue probably could teach what Judaism really meant but nine times out of ten he was overburdened with a host of other synagogue responsibilities.

Thus, the youngsters learned the narrative biblical tales, a few highlights of Jewish history which somehow focused on tragic events such as the destruction of the Holy Temple in 586 BCE, and the second Temple in 70 CE, and the mass expulsion of the Jews from Spain. Rarely were they given a taste of the immortal teachings of *Ethics of the Fathers,* for example, or a summary of the great Jewish personalities—ancient and modern—who succeeded in attaining great achievements in their respective fields of work, while at the same time clinging tenaciously to their Jewish heritage and traditions.

Thus, what happened for many decades was that large numbers of Jewish boys and girls, roughly from the 1930s until today, learned almost nothing meaningful in their afternoon schools. Many left the bar or bat mitzvah ceremony, and the party that followed, and vowed silently that they were "through with all that." And for many years there was very little contact between them and a synagogue.

There was some improvement in the quality of the Jewish education for youths after the end of World War II when Jewish day schools proliferated all over the country. Here the level of Jewish education was relatively high; the student also divided his time between general studies and Jewish studies, so that by virtue of time alone he could not help but enhance his Jewish knowledge. Not all families however were prepared to send their children to an all-day school, a yeshiva. For one thing it was costly, although scholarships were provided for needy children. For another, many parents were not willing to expose their children to strictly Orthodox schools since they themselves were not Orthodox. Some of this resistance was overcome in later years when both the Conservative and Reform movements set up growing numbers of modern all-day schools.

A negative factor that helped advance the growth of the
Jewish day schools was the decline in the quality of the public
school system in many urban centers. Parents had to decide
between sending a child to a public school where violent incidents were known to take place regularly and a yeshiva where
the child might come home and insist that his family turn Orthodox.

A number of people—fellow congregants, colleagues at
work, neighbors—have asked me if I could recommend a book
to them that would tell them what they could or could not do
as Jews. Better still, what about a Jewish credo?

Regretfully, it is simply not possible to do so. If a Jew is
strictly Orthodox he can turn to the classic *Shulchan Aruch,*
which is a code of Jewish laws and regulations, compiled from
the Bible and the Talmud. It is so filled with rules that there
exists a condensed version of this historic volume, but non-Or-
thodox Jews, and certainly secular Jews, do not feel themselves
bound by its strictures.

Many have tried to write a credo, but it simply has never
caught on. The great philosopher-rabbi-physician Maimonides, who lived about a thousand years ago and who is recognized by virtually all Jews as one of the greatest Jewish figures
of all time, was persuaded to write one, primarily because
great numbers of his fellow Jews—not all of whom were liter-
ate or learned—urged him to do so, for their sake. He finally
agreed and wrote his *Thirteen Principles,* which is found in most
Orthodox and Conservative prayerbooks. But, it has been
placed toward the end, for the fact is that few people pay it any
real attention.

Why? Because, in the words of the great American rabbi
who founded the Reconstructionist wing of Judaism in the
United States, Mordecai M. Kaplan, "Judaism was and is an
evolving civilization—in almost every generation there are
new interpretations, new insights, new commentaries." Thus,
if someone has a religious problem and poses a question to a
handful of rabbis, he will probably receive quite different responses. A great deal of understanding and interpretation

comes from the individual rabbi's personality and approach, for earlier laws and rulings can be restudied and reinterpreted.

The classic example of this is the Jewish law about suicide. The law is very clear: If a Jew commits suicide, which is seen as murder, he may not be buried in a Jewish cemetery. (Some will permit his interment in a far corner of the cemetery, away from the other graves).

A number of years ago an American rabbi, whose congregant appealed to him to reinterpret the law so that his son—a suicide—could be buried in the family plot, studied the matter and came up with a modern solution. He said that the suicide, at the time that he killed himself, was not rational and therefore could not be held responsible for his actions, and thus could be buried in the family plot. Most rabbis nowadays, confronted with the same problem, rule the same way.

There is of course the classic brief explanation of what Judaism is all about. A long time ago, in ancient Judea, the great rabbi Hillel was approached by a pagan. "Tell me, rabbi," he said, "what is Judaism all about? Tell me while I stand on one foot." Hillel did not flinch: "Do not do to others what you would not want them to do to you," he replied. "All the rest is commentary—and now go and study!"

Study, always study, that seems to be the theme of Jewish life. But really, one may ask, how many times can a person read the Bible? Or even the much longer Talmud? A perfectly logical question but one that comes out of not knowing what study means, in a Jewish context.

There are many rabbis and many religious teachers who can take a sentence or two in the Bible, read it aloud to a class, and then explain it, comment on it, interpret it, seek to find the true meaning behind the few words—and turn such a lesson into a two-hour lecture during which no one stirs, and the proverbial pin could be heard falling.

Serious students of Judaica smile knowingly when they say that "the more you read and study, the more you realize how little you really know, and how much more there is to understand in order to approach a semblance of wisdom.

So much for credos. What about other subjects, such as factual questions and factual answers. Do these exist in Judaism? The answer is yes, but one—even here—must bear in mind that some rabbis will not agree. That is why the talmudic tomes are so voluminous: Essentially the talmudic material consists of rabbis discussing biblical points of law, and in most cases a determination is made about what is the proper way to interpret that particular verse in the Bible. But—the dissenting voices of the rabbis who are outvoted are included in the Talmud, so that all serious students can weigh both sides of a discussion, and although there is now a clear-cut decision, the nay-sayers have a chance to be heard too.

It is as though the Supreme Court justices published all of their decisions, and all the discussions, both pro and con, that led up to them, and as though the subjects bruited about ranged across the entire range of human experience. This is analogous to talmudic study.

So, when a rabbi says he's off to study, and he can be seen deeply engrossed in a thick talmudic volume, an onlooker can begin to appreciate the depth of commitment that Judaism has to the concept of learning. A few hundred years ago, when the bulk of Jewry lived in Russia, Poland, Ukraine, Bylerus, and Lithuania, and when most Jews were confined to small hamlets far from centers of culture, they found a great deal of intellectual stimulation in talmudic study, in the study rooms of the local synagogue, surrounded by poverty, often at the mercy of sinister anti-Semites—but comforted in the knowledge that after a day's work they could open a "blat"—a page of the Talmud—and understand the fine points of teaching that the local rabbi was trying to convey.

It was certainly a good way to keep one's mind alert and sharp. (Come to think of it, I have never seen traditional Jews sitting in a synagogue and studying the Talmud who looked as though they might be suffering from Alzheimer's.)

There are many basic differences between Christianity and Judaism. One of the most significant ones begins at birth: A child born to a Christian family is not considered a real Christian until that child is baptized. In Judaism, a child born to a

Jewish mother is automatically Jewish, no ifs, ands or buts. The importance of this is that we Jews are a people, a community that dates back some 4,000 years to Abraham, Isaac and Jacob, who themselves—although they were our Patriarchs—were not privileged to live to receive or to know the great gift of God to the Jewish people, the Torah, the Hebrew Bible.

In a sense Abraham was the first Jew for he voiced belief in the One God and imparted this belief to his son Isaac, and then it became part of Jacob's belief. And there was a covenant between Abraham and God, separate and apart from the covenant between God and the Jewish people which came about when the Torah was handed over to the Jews by Moses. Thus, we are an ancient people and we possess an ancient religious faith. Christians, on the other hand, are a religious body and each new "member" of that faith must first be ushered in via a religious ceremony.

When people think of Einstein, Freud, Ben-Gurion, Jonas Salk, they think of them as Jews, although not one of the aforementioned was a regular worshiper in a synagogue. Nonetheless they thought of themselves as Jews, first and always, and the world thought of them the same way. Judaism is a whole civilization, a lifelong way of life which of course includes its religion and culture.

There are many other fine points of difference between Judaism and Christianity. If a Christian is excommunicated, it is understood that he is being punished by being separated from God. In Judaism, excommunication means something different—you are separated from the community, not from God. A Jew always remains God's child.

Thus, the excommunicated Jew (an extremely rarely invoked punishment) can pray to God alone, in his home; if however he comes to the synagogue, he will not be counted in the *minyan,* the religious quorum—he has been to all intents and purposes cut off from the Jewish community.

It may be difficult for non-Jews to understand this, but the overwhelming majority of American Jews go for months and months without reciting a religious blessing or offering a prayer. They are nonetheless Jews in every sense of the word.

Large numbers of American Jews, both young and old, are proud Jews—proud of the Jewish people's contributions to the world, which are often seen as far out of proportion with our minuscule numbers. When a Jew achieves a medical or scientific breakthrough, we feel almost parental pride, since many remember painfully how a half-century ago we were being slaughtered in Europe by the Nazis, and no one lifted a hand to help us. On the other hand, when a criminal with a distinctly Jewish name is arrested and found guilty, we heave almost a collective sigh of shame.

Most Jews do not actively think about God per se; somehow we sense that He is there, that we are being watched over by Him, and we remain optimistic that one day, in this still mad, mixed up world, an era of peace and tranquility will descend on all mankind. And that all the Jews who are suffering, and all other people too, will be ushered into a wonderful new time of messianic proportions.

Chapter VII

Is Battle Against Intermarriage Lost?

THERE ARE SOME—NOT MANY—JEWISH COMMUNAL LEADERS who say the fight against intermarriage and the erosion of the American Jewish community is lost, and that all efforts should be directed towards the Christian spouse in an intermarriage to convert to Judaism. This is an open, pluralistic society, these people maintain, and there simply is no way that young Jews can be dissuaded from marrying Christians.

Not all people agree with this assessment. A careful analysis of the most recent data, culled from a 1990 U.S. National Jewish Population Survey—sponsored by the Council of Jewish Federations—turns up some interesting points:

- As of 1985, fully 52 per cent of Jewish men and women who married took non-Jews as spouses.
- No fewer than 75 percent of the children of intermarried couples (without conversion) are being raised as Christians, or without any religious affiliation or teaching at all.
- Of the intermarried couples, only 5 per cent have had the Christian partner convert to Judaism (either before or after the marriage took place).
- Contrary to public opinion, far more Jews are practicing Christianity than has hitherto been known.
- Of those Christian partners in an intermarriage who converted to Judaism, some 30 per cent—some 50,000 people—have done so without any rabbinical guidance or sanction.
- The number of children born to date of intermarriages has reached the astounding figure of approximately 770,000 (this figure includes couples where a partner has converted to Judaism as well as couples where no such conversion has taken place). Only 28 percent of this 770,000 total are being reared as Jews, 31 percent are being raised without any religious faith at all, and 41 per cent are being raised in another faith, usually Christianity. (In this latter category, a smattering of Jewish customs and holidays are sometimes also observed).

When this report was first released, there were some Jewish leaders who said it was not accurate and indeed was wildly exaggerated. With time, however, virtually everyone in the Jewish community has come to accept this data, disheartening as it may be. Some Orthodox leaders pointed to the figures and insisted they had been right all along, namely, in their view the only sure way to retain Jewish affiliation in the United States was through strict, Orthodox practice and interpretation. Nevertheless, some 93 per cent of American Jews continue to reject Orthodoxy.

One of the revealing bits of data turned up by this survey is that the children of intermarriages—where one partner in the union either did or did not convert to Judaism—have grown up and themselves begun to marry. The intermarriage rate of these children is over 90 per cent.

Thus, it turns out that the children of two Jewish parents seem to wish to marry Jews and continue the traditions of Jewish life, but wishing and doing, of course, are two different things. In America's wide open society, young people go out into the world, meet members of the opposite sex from widely different backgrounds—religion, national origin, social or economic status—and react to their own needs and aspirations when they decide on a marriage partner.

In a somewhat earlier study conducted in Cleveland, often cited as a prototype of the American Jewish community, additional provocative facts came to light:

- Among Orthodox families, at least one child had intermarried; the Orthodox intermarriage rate was 15 percent; in the Conservative families, the intermarriage rate went up to 31 per cent; and among the Reform Jews it rose to 36 per cent.
- Among Jewish families that were not affiliated with any religious institution, the rate of intermarriage skyrocketed to 63 per cent—in other words, some two-thirds of the children of Jewish families that had no ties whatever with a religious body intermarried (not all children in such a family, but at least one such child). The Cleveland study noted that wherever there was parental opposition to intermarriage, lower rates of intermarriage ensued.

Are all or the vast majority of Jewish parents opposed to intermarriage? Actually, a large majority is against such marriages, but for many such families—who are themselves assimilated and feel themselves apart from the bulk of American Jewry—it is a non-issue. "If my son wishes to marry a Gentile girl," they'll say, "that's entirely up to him. We just want him to be happy." Although this is still a minority view, it is not insubstantial.

I remember hearing a lecture on the subject by a woman professor. She and her husband, Orthodox traditional Jews, raised three sons, sent them to yeshiva, maintained a religious,

Jewish-minded home. One day their eldest son came home from college and announced that he was getting married to a Gentile girl. He said he loved her, she was the only woman in the world for him, they would be very happy—it was useless to even try to change his mind, and he wanted his parents to agree to attend the wedding, which would take place in a church.

The parents were upset, naturally, but they refused to do or say anything that might alienate their son from them. With heavy hearts they agreed, and even consented to the marriage being officiated over by a Christian minister. But then the mother—stubbornly and intuitively—made one stipulation. The minister was to make no reference during the ceremony to Jesus. Her son thought it over, and agreed. He said, "that seems like a fair compromise."

He returned home again from college a few weeks later, and announced that the wedding was off. His parents did not wish to show him how happy they were. Matter-of-factly they asked him, "What happened?"

"Her parents insisted that there be no changes in the ceremony, and no omission of the name of Jesus," he said. "Their daughter agreed, we had an argument, and that ended the whole thing."

In another case, the son of a successful Boston businessman, who had given his son no Jewish religious background whatsoever, objected to the young man's announcement that he was soon to be married to a lovely, Gentile girl. The father, a widower, was very unhappy at his son's announcement, and urged that the young man—a brilliant, promising Harvard graduate—visit his friend in New York before taking the final step to marriage.

"He's a religious guy and very knowledgeable about Judaism and such," the father said. "Talk to him, and afterwards you decide." The son agreed; he proceeded to New York, and spent several afternoons with his father's friend, a bank executive who sat in his office wearing a yarmulke, and who talked to the young man for many hours—he gave him a concise course in Jewish religious practice, in Jewish history and philosophy, in all the reasons why he should marry a fellow Jew.

When the informal study sessions were over, the young man thanked the banker, said he had enjoyed learning so much in such a short time, and then said he was still planning to go ahead and marry the Christian girl. The father's friend wished him well and they parted.

The young man returned to the banker's office about two months later.

"Do I owe you a *mazeltov?*" he asked the young man.

"No, no, we didn't get married," he replied.

"Why? What happened?"

Feeling a little foolish, the young man replied: "It was her parents—they raised holy hell about her marrying a Jew."

The principal purpose of his visit, he explained to the banker, was to request a list of books from which he could continue to learn more about Judaism.

One of the results of the survey that showed the high degree of intermarriage in this country and the growth of assimilation that generally results from it has been intensive, almost frantic, efforts on the part of synagogues, rabbis and Jewish organizations to find study materials that will persuade Jewish teenagers and college-age students to focus their marriage plans on Jewish spouses.

One school of thought in the organized Jewish community refuses to accept the inevitability of intermarriage and assimilation in open, democratic societies like that of the United States. These Jewish leaders know very well that intermarriage has been the norm in small, isolated Jewish communities like those of Finland or Venezuela, but insist that in large, sophisticated, strong Jewish communities like that of the United States, buttressed by the existence and moral support of Israel, ways can be found to stem the intermarriage rate.

They also stress the importance of reaching out to the Christian partners in such marriages in a major effort to persuade them to convert to Judaism—for the benefit of their family, and for the sake of unity and harmony within that family.

What has become clear is that those Christian partners in an intermarriage who do convert to Judaism generally become exemplary, devoted and observant Jews, who express great joy for having taken that step. Nevertheless, special efforts must be made to teach the more than 50,000 Christians who announced that they had become Jews, without benefit of rabbinical guidance, teaching or formal religious conversion. Many experts fear that these people will become "one-generation converts" and that their children will not follow them into the Jewish community, since the children—according to Jewish law—are not really Jewish.

There are other issues within the Jewish community that still need to be solved, vis-a-vis the problem of converts. The chief of these is the absence of a uniform conversion law that would be acceptable to all the wings of Judaism. A conversion rite according to Halachah—Jewish religious law—is insisted on by the Orthodox and Conservative branches of Judaism, but not by the Reform. That is why every now and then an immigrant to Israel who had been converted by a Reform rabbi runs into trouble when he or she wishes to marry an Israeli Jew. The Israeli rabbinate, in the overwhelming number of cases, does not accept the validity of a Reform conversion, and thus designates such a marriage between a Reform-converted Jew and an Israeli Jew as adultery.

Since people who arrive in Israel as immigrants already married are not questioned by the rabbinate, many of the couples caught up in such situations simply fly out of the country to a nearby city and are married by a local rabbi or in a civil ceremony.

Experts in the fields of intermarriage hold that grandchildren born to parents where there was no conversion, whose parents also did not convert to Judaism, will be lost to Judaism forever. A study in 1984 in Philadelphia showed that not one such grandchild—after two generations of no-conversion intermarriage—had married a Jew. One must remember the other salient statistic: among intermarried couples where there is no conversion, fully three-fourths of the children are not being raised as Jews.

The overall situation from the Jewish viewpoint is gloomy. If intermarriage without conversion to Judaism continues at its present rapid rate, the size, and therefore the strength and significance, of the Jewish community in America will decline. A new survey taken among Christians does not help the situation: some 83 per cent approve the marriage of their children, or any Christian young people, to Jewish partners. As one Jewish cynic said when he read the 83 per cent statistic, "Halleluyah! We have arrived. Now they want us for in-laws!"

Intermarriage and assimilation have been going on throughout Jewish history. There is hardly any trace of the first Jewish immigrants who came to the United States in the early and late 1700s—most of them simply were absorbed into the larger mainstream. The same thing has been experienced in free societies where Jews felt little need to maintain their traditions and heritage.

I remember once meeting a university professor from Spain, a very pleasant man whose company I enjoyed. I knew, of course, that hundreds of thousands of Jews had been either burned at the stake or expelled from Spain in the late fifteenth century, owing to the religious fanaticism of the Catholic Church of that era. I also knew that hundreds of thousands had hidden their origins, had continued to some extent to observe Jewish customs, and had in all likelihood gradually been integrated into the general population.

My Spanish professor, I thought, looked Jewish—something I could not describe any better. It was just a hunch.

I asked him, "Tell me, if you don't mind my asking—are you Jewish?"

He laughed and answered. "Who knows? By now we are all mixed up."

One of the factors encouraging intermarriage is the all-pervasive television set. Millions, Jews and Christians, watch shows like "L. A. Law" or "Thirtysomething." They see a Jew and a Christian married to one another, they seem to be happy and content. What a message that is for young American Jews!

The only way that a Jew living in modern America can resist intermarriage is first and foremost if he has a determination that the Jewish people—some 4,000 years old, with a long record of vital contributions to society—deserves to continue to exist as an organized community. If one makes that determination about Jewish continuity, out of positive motives not jingoism, I believe ways will be found to reduce the rate of intermarriage and also to convince the Christian partner in an existing intermarriage to convert to Judaism.

Anything less would be a disaster for the Jewish people— the six million Jews massacred by the Nazis a half-century ago would be joined by an equal number of Jews in America, who would quietly and painlessly disappear through absorption by the far greater numbers of the Christian populace.

The Jewish people recovered from the Nazis' genocide. The Jewish response to Hitler was to establish Israel and help it flourish, and to build a thriving, successful community in the United States.

The danger of American Jewry's painless disappearance dare not be ignored nor brushed under the rug.

From time to time a Jewish young man or woman, intent on marrying a Christian, and seeking to overcome parental objections will say: "But the Bible doesn't say you should not marry a Gentile!"

Not true. Clearly, unambiguously Chapter 7, verses 3 and 4, of the fifth book of the Hebrew Bible, Deuteronomy, declares: "You shall not marry with your non-Jewish neighbors. Your daughter shall not be given to their son, nor their daughter to your son. For intermarriage will turn children away from Judaism, and they will end up serving other religions."

There are other biblical citations strongly opposing intermarriage, including a passage in Exodus (34:16), and also in Kings I, Nehemiah, Malachi—not to mention the frequent admonitions found in the Talmud, and in other sacred Jewish texts through the centuries.

Some will say that prohibiting intermarriage is narrow-minded vis-a-vis Gentiles. Again this is not true. On the contrary, the Bible and all Jewish sacred literature constantly urges Jews to extend fair treatment to their non-Jewish neighbors; the values often voiced in the Torah are intended not for Jews alone but for all peoples, they are truly universal. But, and this is a big but, if Jews intermarry, the sages immediately understood, then the Jewish people per se will disappear. The continuity of the Jewish community needs and requires endogamy, marriage within the group. This is seen as nothing less than a matter of Jewish survival.

Then there are the young Jews eager to marry a non-Jew who will point to Moses and Joseph, and argue that these great Jewish personalities married Gentiles. This has been cited before, indeed for many centuries. The response is simple— both Moses and Joseph lived in non-Jewish environments, and there were no singles dances where they could meet eligible young Jewish women. That is exactly one of the points being stressed—namely, that Jewish young men and women should live in places where they can meet and eventually marry. All those Jews who, for whatever reason, lived apart from the Jewish community eventually married non-Jews, and were usually lost to the Jewish people.

One has but to think of the young progenitor of the Goldwater family who went west in the 1800s to make his fortune. His name at the time was Goldwasser; he worked diligently and built a business in Arizona, and when he married he felt he had no choice but to select a Christian girl from the area. They married and raised a family; the distinguished United States senator, Barry Goldwater, points proudly to his roots, but he and his family are all Christians. There were hundreds, perhaps thousands, of similar cases as the West was settled and won.

Or think of the situation that existed in Czarist Russia 150 years ago. Conscription was the law of the land; Jewish boys were no exception, and in most cases they were taken into the Russian army at the age of fourteen, and had to serve for 25 years. Many, of course, perished as a result of the harsh conditions under which they were forced to live. But those who survived, and were finally discharged past the age of forty, no longer thought of themselves as Jews. Some had married or lived with Russian peasant women who lived near the army bases. The cruelties of military life in czarist Russia at the time drove their Jewishness out of them; they too were lost to the Jewish people, and to their families.

Thus, when Abraham decided it was time to find a suitable wife for his son Isaac, he sent his trusted servant Eliezer to find a young woman among his family. And later, when it was time for Rebecca and Isaac's son Jacob to get married, Rebecca also expressed her fears that Jacob would marry a Gentile girl.

Sometimes a stubborn youth, determined to overcome parental opposition to his or her marital choice, will suggest that the parents allow the marriage to go forward, and then later the Gentile partner will convert to Judaism. Actually, it is a good argument, for many born Jews know that by and large the "Jews by Choice," i.e., the converts, in almost all cases turn out to be exceptional members of the Jewish community. However, this procedure generally does not work.

It is quite a different story if the would-be convert willingly agrees to study with a rabbi who will instruct that person in basic Judaism, and agrees also (if he's a man) to undergo either a circumcision, or at least a symbolic circumcision. Nor must there be any hesitation on the part of the convert to throw in his lot with the Jewish people, fully and totally, including raising a Jewish family, observing the religious laws and traditions, joining a synagogue, in short, agreeing to become a full-fledged Jew before the wedding, without any equivocation. Anything less than such a commitment waters down the whole conversion process, and is seen to be an expedient, insincere undertaking.

Then there are Jewish youths who approach the rabbi and ask, if the would-be spouse rejects conversion, "Rabbi, can't I get married and then if there are children, I'll raise them as Jews?" This too may be seen as a strong argument, especially if the mother-to-be is Jewish, and she knows the Jewish law, namely, that a child born to a Jewish mother is automatically Jewish.

But this also falls flat, in the face of the factual data: 72 per cent of the children born in intermarriages, where the Gentile partner has not converted, are reared as Gentiles. The so-called dual religious household that some intermarrieds espouse is based on a false premise; where both Judaism and Christianity are taught in that household, a 1983 survey by Dr. Egon Mayer shows, the overwhelming majority of support goes to the Christian side. After all, by far the overwhelming majority of people in this country are Christians. Why shouldn't we expect a young child to be influenced by this environment? Indeed, when Mayer posed the question to children in these dual religion homes, *Do you feel a greater responsibility to Jews in need than to others in need,* 83 per cent said no.

Another little-appreciated statistic arose when in-depth studies were made of intermarried couples when there had been no conversion. A survey in the 1980s showed that a married couple where both partners are Jewish had a 15 per cent chance of being divorced, while in an intermarriage, again where there was no conversion, the divorce rate climbed to between 40 and 50 per cent.

The late Paul Cowan, a born Jew who had had almost no exposure to Jewish life, married Rachel Cowan, who was a Gentile. After a few years, as Rachel decided to convert to Judaism and Paul became more and more observant and committed to a Jewish lifestyle, they came to the realization that couples who were intermarried without benefit of a conversion faced what they called "time bombs"—religious situations that were just waiting to blow up.

Included among these "time bombs" were visits to grandparents, one set Christian and the other Jewish, where the children were exposed to opposing customs, beliefs and values. If a little boy was born to the couple, would they argue about a *brit* (a religious circumcision) or a baptism? How would the major Jewish and/or Christian holidays be celebrated? How would the children feel if there were no holidays celebrated in that particular home?

The Cowans asked more pointed questions: If there were a film depicting the horrors of the Holocaust, and if the Jewish grandparents were present, how would they respond if the children referred to "those people" and not "our people?"

A Christmas tree festooned with Christian symbols in an intermarried home where there was no conversion is guaranteed to irritate the Jewish partner. And perhaps the Chanukah candles will equally disturb the Christian spouse.

In the 1990 National Jewish Population Survey, it was estimated that more than 200,000 born Jews in the United States have converted to other religions, or have become associated with cults such as Jews for Jesus, Scientology, Born Again Christianity. They no longer consider themselves Jews and for all practical purposes they are not.

In addition, according to the same study, more than 1,000,000 born Jews in America no longer consider themselves members of a religious faith. Most of these people are intermarried to Gentiles, and have decided that the easiest way to cope with the problem is to become a full-fledged secularist. Religion is no longer part of their life. They believe in nothing.

At times these intermarried "secular" Jews claim to be "cultural Jews"—whatever that means.

I chuckle when I hear this, recalling the comment made by the late Harry Wolfson, professor of philosophy at Harvard for many years. He was once asked his religion and replied: "I am a non-practicing Orthodox Jew."

Chapter VIII

Hatred's History Looms in Shadows

RABBI ALAN SILVERSTEIN HAS WRITTEN A BRIEF BUT INCISIVE
brochure on the accelerating problem of intermarriage confronting the American Jewish community entitled "Intermarriage: Our Grounds for Concern," in which he asks and then
answers fourteen basic questions on the issue.

One of these questions is by a hypothetical Jew contemplating marriage to a Christian, who has rejected conversion to Judaism and who has no plans to raise any future children in the
Jewish faith. Under these circumstances, the questioner asks,
"I assume that my own Judaism will nevertheless remain
intact."

To which Rabbi Silverstein responds in the negative. Noting that the growing number of Jews in the United States who "no longer consider themselves Jews" and who do not follow any religious path—they are estimated at over one million—Silverstein points to the fact that many of these are intermarried with spouses who did not join the Jewish community. In addition, the rabbi points out that more than 200,000 Jews have converted out of Judaism and are members of other religious groups (notably Christian denominations, but also various cults that call themselves religious groups); he cautions that the Jewish partner caught up in such an intermarriage will—in the words of the Bible—"serve other religions."

He writes: "Intermarriage not only removes future generations from the Jewish fold, it also leads to the gradual erosion of the Jewish identity of the mixed married Jew. Although exceptions exist, a gradual process of alienation is greatly to be feared . . . simply considering oneself as 'nothing' (religiously) leads the intermarried Jew not only to be uninvolved in synagogue and Jewish communal life—it is frequently also accompanied by a distancing from Jewish friends and Jewish family members."

Rabbi Silverstein's insightful pamphlet was published by the United Synagogue of Conservative Judaism, as was another recommended brochure written by that organization's executive vice-president, Rabbi Jerome Epstein, titled "A Return to the Mitzvah of Endogamy."

There are some leaders of the Jewish community who believe that one quick and easy way to battle intermarriage is simply to announce that the wives/husbands of intermarrieds (and their children) who have not formally converted to Judaism will henceforth be fully accepted into the synagogue, and into Jewish life in general. Such a policy, they maintain, will gradually impact positively on these non-Jews and in the course of time they will of their own volition convert to Judaism.

At the present time, while most synagogues accept intermarried families as members, the non-Jewish partner in most cases is not accorded any religious honors, such as being called to the Torah on the Sabbath and holidays and similar functions.

The suggestion that the rules be relaxed is rejected by most rabbis. As Rabbi Epstein writes,

> Judaism is a faith community . . . (they) are not simply social settings in which all fine, decent human beings can participate fully and equally. Just as certain civic privileges are available only to American citizens, so too are certain sacred rites of all major religions only made available to members of the faith.
>
> Relatives of faith community members should be made welcome in both synagogues and churches, but religious distinctions still remain. A non-Christian does not receive sacred "communion" rites nor formally come to be regarded as a faith "member" of a church, even though he/she may attend services, adult education classes, social functions and other church gatherings.
>
> Similar principles apply in synagogues. To act otherwise is to redefine a synagogue as a social club, equally accessible to all, regardless of faith commitments and not as an American style faith community.
>
> To involve Christian spouses and children in Jewish services, adult education lectures, family social gatherings, and the like, is praiseworthy. However, to enable practicing Christians or other non-Jews to participate as if they were Jews in Jewish ritual settings, in Jewish leadership levels within the synagogue, is to create confusion in the minds of all concerned. In addition, it blurs the critical distinction between converts and born Jews from non-Jewish relatives of Jewish synagogue members.

In my own synagogue one frequently sees non-Jewish guests on a Sabbath morning when, generally, there is a "simcha," a happy event—a bar or bat mitzvah, a baby-naming (for a girl, since a newborn boy is given his name at the circumcision ceremony), or an *aufruf*, when a groom-to-be is called to the Torah on the eve of his wedding.

Inevitably it becomes clear that the Christian guests are fascinated by what they see and hear. All male visitors when they enter the premises are handed a yarmulke; the prayer shawl, the *tallit,* however is reserved for the Jewish attendees, since it is considered a Bible-ordained religious garment.

The distinctions between Jews and non-Jews at religious services need to be clear; although most Jews warmly welcome the Jews by Choice—those who converted to Judaism and have become part of our community, and these "new Jews" are regarded fully and totally as Jews—they also respect the wishes of Christians, who prefer in effect to remain "Christians by Choice." Coercion is simply not a Jewish tenet.

Parents of teenagers are often confronted by the question of dating a non-Jewish classmate. The Jewish teen generally makes the point that "we're only friends," but is usually unaware of the emotional ties that can be created, willingly or otherwise. In the 1990s many Jewish parents must try to guide their teen-age children away from group dating and solo dating if they wish their children to meet and eventually marry only someone of the Jewish faith. Some teenagers accuse their parents, in heated moments, of being racists and jingoists—which, of course, is silly. The Jewish people is not a race, and does not look down on racial, religious or nationality groups. There are Jews who are of color, and who stem from all kind of national backgrounds; few, if any can trace their lineage to the biblical period.

The only thing that all Jews who are committed to the continuity of the Jewish people want is for the Jewish people to continue to exist and thrive as a recognizable group, playing its part in the symphony of mankind. We believe that the disappearance of the Jews—through Nazi-type massacres or benign assimilation—would be a tragic loss for all mankind.

That is why interdating is strongly opposed by Jews who care about the Jewish future, and why the Jewish community as a whole is seeking every conceivable way to prevent intermarriage and assimilation.

Another argument that frequently surfaces on the part of young American Jews goes something like this: Why is it so important to be Jewish or Christian or even a member of another religion? When all is said and done, don't all these religions have the same goal in mind—that all people should be better, more ethical? Why do we need these labels?

It is certainly true that Judaism and Christianity both have similar goals in mind for their followers. But Jews cannot help but remember how much suffering Jews endured through the ages as a result of Christian religious teaching. For some two thousand years, Jews were charged with killing Jesus (the crime of deicide), they were charged with murdering small Christian children in order to use their blood in the baking of matza for Passover, they were described in church sermons and religious texts as friends of Satan, and thus cohorts of the devil. Anti-Semitic charges included the laughable statements that we controlled the world's economy, the international media, the political machines, and thus are really the cause of all the world's problems. This hatred of Jews, unfortunately, remains imbedded in the minds and hearts of millions of Christians. The Vatican, as is known, sought to remove this anti-Jewish hatred by deleting all anti-Semitic charges from church services and textbooks; to a large extent this has been a successful program.

Nevertheless, anti-Jewish bigotry from the right and the left has continued in many parts of the world, especially where economic or political turmoil arose, encouraging people in distress to seek a scapegoat to blame for their troubles—and, as has been the case for nearly two millenia, Jews have been readily available as targets for blind hatred, coupled with insane charges.

In Chicago, for example, a Black anti-Semitic minority group actually claimed that Jewish doctors were deliberately spreading the AIDS virus among the Black population; tragically, there were people gullible enough to believe even so monstrous a story.

Can a Jew and a Christian intermarry, both knowing that this pattern and history of anti-Jewish violence and prejudice exists, and has existed for many centuries, and live together amicably, lovingly, with this memory in the background? Can a Jew and a Christian intermarry bearing in mind that Jews do not believe that Jesus was the Messiah and recalling that Christianity teaches that all those who do not believe in Jesus as the Messiah will be condemned to hell?

Another way to distinguish the major differences between Judaism and Christianity: Judaism basically is a religion of deeds, with commandments that teach that one must do as much as possible to carry out these good deeds on God's earth; while Christianity insists that all people must have total faith in Jesus. Can two people coming from two such separate and diverse backgrounds find a common ground that will provide a lifetime of stability, love and serenity for themselves and their children?

So, when parents object to interdating and intermarriage, many of these issues are in the back of their minds, and in their memory although not always are they capable of expressing them.

Is it true, some Jewish teens ask, that rabbis are far more opposed to intermarriage than their colleagues, the Christian ministers? Certainly. It is simply a matter of numbers. The marriage of young Christians to young Jews in America is numerically insignificant from a Christian standpoint. But from a Jewish standpoint, it is a major issue—surely the most pressing issue challenging all thoughtful American Jews.

What Jews in the United States say among themselves is that during the years of the Nazi era, no fewer than six million Jews were murdered—a full third of the world's Jewish population. In free, democratic America, they muse, there could be—God forbid!—a "silent Holocaust," in which millions of Jews slip away from Judaism and the Jewish community, and slip gently into the mainstream Christian community. Such a loss, Jews feel, would be irreplaceable; and although the Jewish people have been around for some 4,000 years, surviving all kinds of attacks, pogroms, expulsions, the disappearance of large numbers of American Jews peacefully and quietly would be too great a blow. It could well be the end of the Jewish people and the end of Jewish history.

I am reminded of the late Eric Hoffer, a German-born longshoreman who worked on the docks of California and became one of America's most gifted philosophers. He wrote that as far as he was concerned, the condition of the Jews is a barometer of the world as a whole. If, he wrote, Heaven forbid, the Jews disappear because of intermarriage, cults and Christian missionaries, then who knows if the world has a future at all.

Then, in sum, why are rabbis so much more firmly opposed to intermarriage than the Christian clergymen? Because the latter are concerned with their major problem, which in America in the 1990s is the growing secularization of the new generation. Jews who marry Christians and join the mainstream community are a very minor equation in Christian religious thinking.

The situation can be compared to Israel where 85 percent of the population is Jewish, while most of the remainder is Moslem. Christians are barely one percent, and that is why they strive to maintain their religious identity and institutions, so that they will not be integrated into the majority Jewish (and Moslem) cultures.

Teenagers and college-age students who wish to marry a Gentile are caught on the proverbial horns of a dilemma. They don't wish to upset their parents, or disappoint their family's rabbi, or alienate themselves from siblings and other relatives—but they are persuaded that they are in love, and that the person of their affectionate attentions is the only one who will make them happy, and that, somehow, things will work out, all the obstacles will be overcome peacefully and without rancor.

Thus, after heated discussions, arguments, debates, probably tears, the young person in question finally asks: All right, we're both talking on totally different wavelengths. So, tell me—a parent or a rabbi or a religious teacher is finally asked—why should I remain Jewish? Why do I need the extra burden? Isn't choosing a life partner, and a career, and making a life for myself all a tough enough job? Why do I have to complicate my life with this Jewish thing?

Rabbi Philmore Berger of Long Island responds to the provocative question with an immediate, almost terse reply: Because Judaism believes in *tikkun olam,* fixing and improving the world. That is the role of Jews, and that is more than enough reason to be actively and proudly Jewish. Rabbi Ephraim Rubinger, also of Long Island, replies differently: Because Judaism is a way of life that brings in its wake serenity, harmony, and true joy; because it is a faith that is logical, insightful and wise; and because it would be a betrayal of my parents and grandparents, and their parents all the way back, if I were to sever the link in the chain that stretches across four millenia of Jewish history. Rabbi Alan Silverstein of New Jersey answers as follows: Because

> We owe it to God (with Whom) we have a convenental bond to represent ethical monotheism in this world . . . We owe it to our ancestors (who) kept alive the unbroken chain of tradition, sometimes at great peril to their lives, to pass this precious legacy on to the next generation . . . some of our ancestors may have been pious and others secular but each . . . recognized that unless they passed the baton on to the next in line, they would deny their sons and daughters and grandchildren the opportunity to choose whether or not to be intimately involved in the riches of Jewish ritual, values, learning, wisdom, and spirituality . . . we owe it to our fellow Jews of today . . . we owe it to the world. Judaism and the Jewish people have made profound contributions to world culture, science and ethics far in excess of our tiny numbers . . . we owe it to ourselves to remain Jewish—Judaism is a fantastic religious approach to every facet of our lives. Converts to Judaism are quick to point out the blessings of Judaism.

In a wonderfully provocative book published nearly twenty years ago, *The Nine Questions People Ask about Judaism,* by Dennis Prager and Joseph Telushkin, they write to Jews who stand on the threshold of abandoning the Jewish faith and/or the Jewish community as follows: "You may be able to judge the Judaism of your parents and/or the Judaism of your local Temple, but the Judaism which has survived 3,500 years, the Judaism which bequeathed to the world God and universal morality, the Judaism which survived Pharoah, Rome, the Crusades . . . Hitler and Stalin, and the Judaism which today puts the Jewish people at the vortex of human affairs, is the authentic and powerful Judaism of which, sadly, you might know very little."

A number of scholars of the development of the American Jewish community take a less pessimistic view of the future of American Jewry than do some of their colleagues. They note, correctly, that while the rate of intermarriage is extremely high, the figures are somewhat distorted: The children born to intermarrieds where there was no conversion, or even where there was a conversion to Judaism, tend to intermarry at an extremely high rate, while the children of couples who are both born Jews seem to prefer inmarriages, i.e., marriages to fellow Jews, although here too the rate of intermarriage continues to mount as the years progress, and as the integration of American Jews goes forward. Sociologists like to point out that there is a great difference between integration and assimilation, the latter implying that the character of the Jewish community—its distinctiveness and uniqueness—is gradually but steadily becoming blurred by the overwhelming size of the larger community that is in effect swallowing up the smaller.

Some Jews like to say that interdating and even intermarriage indicate that Jews have finally reached a position where they are fully accepted as compatriots of their non-Jewish fellow Americans. This sounds too much like rationalizing; as though to be really accepted by the larger Christian population, we must surrender our religion, our way of life, our culture. Indeed, I believe the opposite is true: Christians will intuitively have greater respect for Jews who display an inner and outer esteem for their own faith than for Jews who observe very little of their own ancient faith, and who know very little about it when they are questioned.

In the half-century that has passed from the 1940s to the 1990s, the American Jewish community has been transformed radically. In the '40s, Jews in America were fearful that Nazism would spread to the United States; there were strong efforts to promote American Nazism and virulent anti-Semitism. In those years, few Jews could afford to attend college out of town and thus few had occasion to meet non-Jewish fellow students. Intermarriage for Jews was so rare, it was a non-issue.

When World War II ended in 1945, and Israel was established in 1948, Jews began to change. The Holocaust shocked them into the knowledge that Jews could be massacred with impunity. Israel's courageous military stance in her embryonic years of statehood gave every Jew in the world a new sense of self-esteem. And tens of thousands of World War II Jewish veterans in the United States began to take advantage of American government support for a college education, and for purchasing a low-cost home in the suburbs.

Within two decades, the face of American Jewry changed: large numbers of children, emulating their fathers, attended out-of-town colleges; now they met and socialized with Gentiles, and some fell in love. The intermarriage cauldron began to stir. Their parents in the suburbs built a large number of impressive synagogues, and added to the traditional prayerbooks prayers for the well-being of Israel, and memorial prayers for the six million Jews who had been killed by the Nazis.

Without articulating the words, Jews vowed that "never again" would there be another Holocaust. They sought to live more Jewish lives by some form of close association with the local synagogue and with a wide range of Jewish organizations that worked diligently for many different goals. Jewish religious schooling grew, especially in the area of all-day schools. Bar and bat mitzvah celebrations were featured almost every Sabbath in every part of the country, and Gentile friends were generally invited.

And then the fly appeared in the ointment—the young Jews who had been proudly sent off to prestigious colleges began to return with Gentile boyfriends and girlfriends. Parents were taken aback and shocked. Beginning in the 1960s the problem of intermarriage began to fester, and now, in the 1990s, has become a critical issue for the Jewish community.

One of the most activist rabbis against intermarriage and apathy is associated with the Lincoln Center Synagogue in

New York City. In an interview in *Newsweek,* Rabbi Ephraim Buchwald said: "Intermarriage is a death knell . . . there has never been a community of Jews that abandoned ritual and survived."

Steven Bayme, a Jewish community specialist, associated with the American Jewish Committee, was also interviewed by *Newsweek.* He said "We are very good at telling the State Department what to do about Israel, but in the privacy of our homes we cannot find the words to tell our children why they should be Jewish."

American Judaism basically lacks an ideology, Bayme says. "There is a combination of vague pro-Israelism, nostalgia, fear of anti-Semitism, and liberal universalism that we dress up in Jewish garb . . . Jews want Jewish grandchildren, but only a religious commitment in its various formulations provides a strong ideological rationale for opposing mixed marriages. Only about 20 percent of American Jews are seriously religious (half of these are Orthodox). When parents complain about a forthcoming mixed marriage, and ask 'What did I do wrong?' the answer is they sent their kids to Sunday school—while they went shopping or to the beauty parlor."

Bayme's comments about religious observance and instruction and their relationships to intermarriage are borne out by the statistics. Reform Jews, ostensibly the least observant of traditional Jewish rituals and rulings, concede that of all current intermarriages in America, 65 percent take place within their ranks, compared to 50 percent among the Conservative—whose degree of observance is closer to the Orthodox—and 25 percent among the Orthodox.

A prominent article in an Israeli newsmagazine, *Jerusalem Report,* carried some scare headlines: AMERICA'S VANISHING JEWS. INTERMARRIAGE THREATENS THE WORLD'S LARGEST COMMUNITY. What has Israeli leaders, as well as American Jewish leaders, deeply worried is the inescapable fact that since 1985, one of every two marriages involving a Jewish spouse was with a Christian partner. As of today, one-fourth of all married American Jews are wed to non-Jews. Of these mixed couples, only 28 percent are raising their children as Jews. This phenomenon of a rapid intermarriage rate is appreciated when it is compared to the rate of 1960, when only 6 percent of Jews were married to Gentiles.

Another interesting point brought out by the 1990 population survey claims that while there are a total of 3.2 million American Jewish households, only 57 percent of them, or 1.8 million, are comprised of Jews living with Jews. The situation, claimed an Orthodox rabbi, is a catastrophe. "The figures are shocking, and they will become even more shocking," Rabbi Pinhas Stolper declared. "The intermarriage process will take everything Jewish in its wake. It will grow and grow until it engulfs the entire community—it's a Holocaust."

One of the surprising aspects of the overall situation is a sociological sub-study that was made of the population survey. According to Gary Tobin of Brandeis University who studied the intermarriage data painstakingly, there is almost no relationship between increased Jewish learning and a decrease in intermarriage. This odd piece of information applies to Jews under the age of 45, indicating that passion overrules religious education.

What was clear from the study was that a decisive factor in the intermarriage rate was the number of generations that a Jewish family has lived in the United States—the longer a Jew resided in America, the more rooted were his parents, grandparents and great grandparents in American life, the more likely it was that he would intermarry. The children of recent arrivals were thus seen to be the least likely to marry a non-Jew.

Another interesting point developed by the population survey was that—contrary to conventional wisdom—the more educated an individual was, the less likely he was to intermarry. And the more affluent, the less likely an individual was to marry a Christian. One possible explanation for this offered by one specialist, is that being Jewish is expensive—synagogue dues, all-day school tuition, donations to the United Jewish Appeal and other charities add up, and poorer Jews intermarry so as to avoid embarrassment of their lack of funds.

Chapter IX

Questions of the Ages vs. Intermarriage

MANY JEWS, YOUNG AND OLD, WHEN CONFRONTED WITH OB-
jections to intermarriage or assimilation into the larger American culture come up with questions that at first glance
sometimes seem difficult to answer. These questions, all too
often, are designed not so much to enter into a provocative intellectual discussion, but rather to support an already arrived
at opinion.

These questions sometimes sound like philosophical problems that have been asked for many centuries, and for which
there are no easy answers. They are worth exploring, however,
first, to show the questioner that Judaism is not afraid to

tackle tough issues, and secondly because young Jews posing
these questions should not think for a moment that Judaism
squelches open discussion.

One of the perennial problems that generally arises in such
discussions—where parents and/or grandparents are trying to
dissuade a young person from marrying out of the Jewish
faith—is the old one: Why are there Jews who seem to be actively religious but who are really unethical, while at the same
time there are ethical people who are totally irreligious?

Rabbi Milton Steinberg, the author of *Basic Judaism,* who
died in his prime was confronted with that question. His reply
went like this:

> How is one to account for the goodness of so many irreligion-
> ists? Very simply. Men often behave better than their philoso-
> phies. They cannot be expected to persist in doing so. In the end,
> how a man thinks must affect how he acts: atheism must finally,
> if not in one generation, then in several, remake the conduct of
> atheists in the light of its own logic.

Of course, the original error in this question can be seen in
the wording of the problem. The word "religious" is all
wrong; a "religious" Jew is one who carefully follows the ethical and moral laws. A Jew who observes the rules dealing with
kosher food, or the Sabbath, or holidays, and the like, may be
described as following Jewish ritual practices. To be ethical in
Jewish tradition one has to be compassionate, patient, kind,
honest, and always bear in mind the talmudic advice that one
should not judge another until "you are in his place."

A Jew at services who prays loudly is not regarded as more
"religious" than a silent worshiper. Quite the contrary, he
may, by his noisy praying, be trying to smother a guilty conscience. Judaism is very explicit about what makes an ethical
person: giving charity, helping the poor, never cheating, not
mistreating an employee, avoiding gossip, not taking revenge
or bearing a grudge, not standing idly by while someone's
blood is being shed.

In short, following the simple maxim that is found high up

on the wall of many synagogues, facing the congregation: V'AHAVTA L'RAY'ACHA CAMOCHA, Love your neighbor as yourself. That is ethical behavior.

As for the irreligious—or even atheistic—person who is ethical: There are certainly many people who are born with high moral principles, or else they have inherited these from parents or grandparents, or even from the great religious teachings of the ages, even though they do not acknowledge or subscribe to them.

One must ask such a person how he plans to pass on to the next generation his own admirable ethical behavior? Setting an example for a child is certainly an excellent method, but if the whole world is replete with unethical goings-on, how is that young person to be safeguarded from being influenced by these unethical factors if not for religious teaching?

The Bible cautions us that a man's heart is evil from his youth—and must therefore be molded morally and ethically. Anarchy will reign if law and morality are shunted aside. The philosopher Will Herberg, in his book *Judaism and Modern Man,* said the "moral principles of western civilization are all derived from the tradition rooted in Scripture . . . morality ungrounded in God is a house built upon sand, unable to stand up against the vagaries of impulse and the brutal pressures of power and self-interest."

Thus, an irreligious ethical person, whether he wishes to acknowledge it or not, owes a great debt of thanks to direct or oblique religious teaching. Or, he may be one of the few people born with a fully-developed ethical character. Substituting such beliefs as ethical humanism for religion is self-deluding; history has shown that people need an ethical code to follow, and a firm belief in God in order to advance on the ladder of morality.

Another question often put to parents and rabbis and others by Jewish teens or college students contemplating intermarrying goes something like this: "Okay, both Judaism and Christianity are obviously, clearly faiths that seek to bolster ethical living and behavior, peace and justice in the world, and amity among all peoples—so, where do the two religions really differ? If a Catholic marries a Protestant, nobody makes a fuss—but if I, a Jew, wish to marry a Christian, my family goes bananas. What then is the difference between the two religions?"

This is not a difficult question to respond to—Judaism stresses deeds while Christianity insists on faith in its tenets. Indeed, there are three major Christian dogmas that separate Christianity from Judaism—original sin, the Second Coming, and atonement through Jesus' death. For Christians these acts of faith are needed to solve religious problems that otherwise seem unsolvable. For Jews, however, these problems do not exist, and therefore there is no need for these beliefs.

Judaism does not accept the concept that there is such a thing as "original sin" and that all people are born sinners. On the contrary, we believe that each person is born innocent, and each person, by living his life, becomes either a sinner or a good, even a righteous, person.

The idea of Jesus' Second Coming—to fulfill the prophecies that were not fulfilled while he lived—is also meaningless for Jews, since we do not accept the belief that he was the Messiah in the first place. As for the concept of atonement for Jesus' death, Judaism maintains a totally different view, namely, that each person can obtain salvation through his own actions.

The Christian dogma that people's sins, presumably against other people, can be forgiven through the death of Jesus is diametrically opposed to the Jewish idea that if a person commits a sin against a fellow human being, that person—and only that person—can forgive him. That is why it is not unusual to see, a little while before Yom Kippur, the holiest day of the Jewish calendar, individual Jews approaching fellow Jews and whispering words to the effect: "If I have sinned against you, please forgive me." If the person who is approached says, "All right, I forgive you," then both people feel better, and approach the Yom Kippur fast and holiday with more hope than heretofore. On this holy day, Jewish tradition says God will determine each person's fate for the new year, and seal it in. Before He can forgive someone for a transgression, that person must have already received forgiveness from the person who was injured.

The question as to differences between Judaism and Christianity now seems less semantic or pedantic. There *are* major differences between the two faiths, and an honest questioner must be prepared to accept an honest reply.

In this context, a question that is often cited by young Jews goes like this: All right, but really, Jesus was a Jew, indeed he was a Jewish teacher—Christians do not deny that. Some even call him "rabbi." Now, then, why don't Jews put an end to anti-Semitism, bigotry, massacres and agree that Jesus was the Messiah?

The question is a logical one, and the answer is because in Jewish tradition and teaching, and, of course, in the ancient prophecies, the advent of the Messiah will usher in an era of peace throughout the world, and the Jewish people will be able to reside peacefully and securely in Israel. Such a time has not arrived, of course. Instead of universal tranquility, there is worldwide tension, wars, disasters, plagues, famine. How can we accept this state of affairs as a hoped for, longed for, prayed for messianic age?

Perhaps a little chastened by now, our young questioner—still intent on intermarrying, and still seeking a logical reason for doing so—may now ask: All right, so please tell me, what is the role that Judaism sees for Jews in this world? And don't tell me about monotheism—that was a great contribution that Jews made, but that was a long time ago, and it has been accepted by Christianity, Islam, and other faiths. What about now, and in the future? What should the goals of the Jewish people be?

The proper answer lies in the Jewish prayerbook, where committed Jews are instructed to declare three times daily (at morning, afternoon and evening prayers) that the mission of the Jewish people is to "perfect the world under the rule of God."

In other words, in a very real sense, although we believe that God created the world, He did not finish the job—we are to be God's co-creators, finishing, improving, repairing—together making this a better world for all people, under God's sovereignty. Since the Torah was given to the Jewish people some 3,500 years ago at Mount Sinai, we have as a people been imbued with the ideas of universal brotherhood, one God, one moral law for all of mankind—and in essence, that remains the mission of Jews to this day.

It should be stressed here that God's choosing the Jews to carry out His wishes was never seen by Jews as giving them extra prestige or privileges—quite the opposite, it means that Jews feel they have an added, special responsibility—in short, an extra burden that we accept since it is God-given, and that many times in our history we have found tiring and difficult.

Twenty-five years ago the editors of *Commentary* magazine asked a group of distinguished rabbis and theologians for their individual views of Judaism's basic concepts and to assess these as they relate to the times in which we live. The impetus for the questions at that time was the often-quoted line that "God is dead;" that quotation has all but disappeared as formal religion has continued to widen its influence, to some extent as an expression of opposition to cults and missionaries, and also, I think, because people have come to believe that living in this world in this time without any faith whatsoever is an extremely difficult thing to do.

How these rabbis and theologians would have reacted to the questions in light of the growth of assimilation and intermarriage is a matter of speculation. The questions submitted to the rabbis dealt with very fundamental issues: Do you believe the Torah to be divine revelation? How do you understand the concept of Jews being God's Chosen People? Is Judaism the only true religion, or are there others too? What distinguishes Jews from Christians in the sphere of ethics? Can a Jew be a racist, a fascist, a communist, and a practicing Jew, all at the same time? What aspects of modern thought do you believe pose the most serious challenge to Judaism?

Rabbi Norman Lamm, president of Yeshiva University, the orthodox institution that includes a seminary for the training of Orthodox rabbis, said: "I believe the Torah is divine revelation in two ways . . . it is God-given and godly. By 'God-given' I mean that He willed that man abide in His commandments and that that will was communicated in discrete letters and words. Man apprehends in many ways: by intuition, inspiration, experience, deduction—and by direct instruction. The divine will, if it is to be made known, is sufficiently important for it to be revealed in as direct, unequivocal, and unambiguous a manner as possible, so that it will be understood by the largest number of the people to whom this will is addressed. Hence, I accept unapologetically the idea of the verbal revelation of the Torah. . . . Exactly how this communication took place, no one can say: it is no less mysterious than the nature of the One who spoke. . . *How* God spoke is a mystery; *how* Moses received this message is an irrelevancy. *That* God spoke is of the utmost significance and *what* He said must therefore be intelligible to humans in a human context. . . All of the Torah—its ideas, its laws, its narratives, its aspirations for the human community—lives and breathes godliness."

On the chosenness of Israel, Rabbi Lamm said: "(This) relates exclusively to its spiritual vocation embodied in the Torah . . . whenever it is mentioned in our liturgy, it is always related to Torah or *mitzvot* (religious commandments). This spiritual vocation consists of (being) a *goy kadosh,* a holy nation, and *mamlechet kohanim,* a kingdom of priests—the first term denotes communal separateness or differentness, in order to achieve a collective self-transcendence . . . the second term implies the obligation of this brotherhood of the spiritually elite toward the rest of mankind. (Priesthood is defined by the prophets as fundamentally a teaching vocation).

"The chosenness of Israel (means that) Israel may be a reluctant teacher and the world an unwilling pupil . . . the teaching occurs on many levels, and is expressed in many ways: by word, by sublime example, and most notably by the very mystery of Jewish history."

On the question of extremist political positions such as fascism or communism Rabbi Lamm says: "They . . . offend human dignity and strip men of certain human rights (and are) obviously in violation of the principles of Judaism. . . I do not believe that Judaism commits us to any specific social, political or ideological system."

Ira Eisenstein, one of the founders of the Reconstructionist movement in Judaism, which basically seeks to separate Jewish thought and observance from the "supernatural," describes Judaism as "the evolving religious civilization of the Jewish people." The "origins of the Jewish people," he says, "are lost in antiquity . . . from earliest times until the end of the eighteenth century Jews believed that the Torah was divine revelation, that the Jewish people was God's 'chosen people' and that all human history revolved around God's relations with Israel: God was either punishing Israel for her sins and hence causing other nations to invade the land and exile the Jews or God was rewarding Israel for obedience, and hence causing the nations to suffer defeat at Israel's hands.

"Since exile was, after the first century of the Christian era, the common lot of Jews, they assumed that they had not expiated their sins; but they believed that any day now God might send the Messiah-king of the royal family of David to redeem them from *galut* (exile) and usher in the messianic age. Then the dead would be resurrected, the final judgment would take place, and the righteous would enter into the world-to-come to enjoy their reward."

Modern historical science has shattered the whole syndrome of these concepts, Eisenstein says. The Torah, he writes, is a "human document, reflecting the attempt of its authors to account for the history of the Jewish people, and for the moral and ethical insights, which its geniuses acquired during the course of that history. It is 'sacred literature' in the sense that Jews have always seen in it the source and the authority for that way of life and that view of history which gave meaning and direction to their lives. . . . For me, those concepts and values explicitly conveyed or implied in the Torah represent discovery, partial and tentative glimpses into the true nature of human life. . . . Some of these ideas, that man is created in the image of the divine, that life is sacred, that man is his brother's keeper, that society must be ruled by law, that justice and compassion are the highest virtues, that moral responsibility is the most authentic form of ethics, that man must serve as a 'partner to God' in perfecting this world, have exerted a tremendous influence on western civilization. . . . I believe that Jews as a people have an opportunity to make a contribution to society that is uniquely their own."

The chancellor of Bar-Ilan University in Israel, Rabbi Emanuel Rackman, said that "a Jew dare not live with absolute certainty, not only because certainty is the hallmark of the fanatic, and Judaism abhors fanaticism, but also because doubt is good for the human soul, its humility, and consequently its greater potential ultimately to discover its Creator.

"Though I remain a creature of doubts, I believe not only that God is, but that He revealed His will to man, to Jews and non-Jews alike. . . . The most definitive record of God's encounters with man is contained in the Torah. Much of it may have been written by people in different times, but at one point in history God not only made the people of Israel aware of His immediacy but caused to write the eternal evidence of the covenant between Him and His people. . . The Jew must be honest with God and himself and seek to ascertain God's will, not his own. . . When Jews become more knowledgeable in their Jewishness, I hope they will recapture in their personal lives a great amount of autonomy, interpreting and applying cherished source materials even as they continue to rely on centralized authority in most matters affecting persons other than themselves."

Rackman continues, on the subject of chosenness: "My belief that God chose Abraham and his seed for the covenant is no warrant for any feeling of superiority over my fellow men. Abraham, according to the record, was selected because God recognized him to be one who would transmit to his posterity a sense of mission with regard to justice and righteousness. . . . My existence has been ennobled because of the mission I have inherited and which I seek to fulfill. I cannot impose it on anyone other than my children—but anyone who wants to share it is free to do so."

Rackman continues: "The daughter religions of Judaism broke with the mother religion by denigrating the realm of the material. Judaism sought to sanctify and perfect all of it— men and beasts, matter and energy, time and space. . . . There is not an area of life for which Judaism does not have a distinctive message; my Judaism provides me with the one integrating approach—I must fathom God's will on every issue. . . . I have no argument with anyone who does not share my religious commitment. I argue only with those whose ideas or deeds are a threat to the messianic vision . . . the secular humanist is not my enemy. (My enemy) is the Buddhist who will affirm the meaninglessness of life or history. So is the Christian who will induce inordinate feelings of guilt with regard to the natural. So is the Moslem who glorifies war. But none is my enemy as a person. . . . My Judaism only becomes richer as I encounter challenges from other cultures."

The late Rabbi Max Routtenberg, on the question of Judaism's being the sole possessor of the truth, said: "God, in the classical Jewish view, did not speak to Israel or to Israel's prophets alone. To the degree that He communicated with other peoples and prophets, Judaism is not in exclusive possession of the truth. God's truths are universal in nature and hence accessible and available to all peoples of all faiths. Judaism is not the one true religion in the sense that no other religion possesses God's truth.

"The challenge to Judaism comes neither from atheists nor from 'God is dead' theologians; it comes from ethical humanists. Ethical humanism has approximated—without religious ritual and without a belief in God—the deepest and noblest insights of Judaism. Why then the ritual, why the belief in God? The religious answer is based on the belief that man is too fragile a reed of the ethical life. The religionist prefers to anchor his life in the great traditions of his religious heritage and to spin the web of his life with the filaments woven by the Divine Weaver." Routtenberg stresses that the "religionist is at all times sustained by the conviction that he is performing God's will."

Rabbi W. Gunther Plaut, one of the leading Reform spokesmen, says about divine revelation at Sinai:

Revelation precludes my giving assent to the proposition that the Torah (the five books of Moses) is divine revelation. It is the mirror of God's presence but not the presence itself. The mirror is flawed because it is human, it is recapitulation of the essence but not the essence itself . . . but, Torah in the wider meaning—denoting Israel's progressing, ongoing encounter with God—represents what record we have of our people's spiritual reach.

All of Torah, down to our day, wrestles with confrontation and turning away, with what was and what is, with reality and potential, with certainty and doubt. . . The (traditional) 613 commandments are my starting point; I observe what I, listening for the voice, can hear as being addressed to me. What I hear today is not always what I heard yesterday, and tomorrow may demand new *mitzvot* (religious commandments), for I may be capable of new insights, a wider reach.

Is Judaism the one true religion? For a Jew it is: for him the covenant provides the framework of his divine and human relationships. For those outside of the *b'rit* (covenant) there are many other opportunities.

What distinctive contribution can Judaism make to the world? Itself. The Jewish way of serving God is not the only way; it is, for humanity's sake, an *essential* way. The presence of the Jew and his tradition, his mood, his stance, his special accent on life—all these have a pivotal role in the society of men. The believing Jew sees himself as a child of the covenant; that he does so as an individual and as a member of a people gives his striving a unique dimension. The believing Jew is always engaged in the salvation of the world rather than of his own soul; in doing so he pursues *mitzvot* rather than proclaiming a system of thought.

Judaism has something to say on all political matters which involve moral judgments. Like everyone else, the Jew ought to make his decisions out of the moral imperatives that govern his life. I act on the basis of Judaism, as I understand it. (Then) could a "good Jew" be a Communist or a Fascist? No, if such political conviction endorses the policy of preventing a man from fulfilling his potential; no, if it means favoring the abridgment of human rights in any form; no, if the interests of the community by definition and practice submerge the liberties of the individual.

I suspect that the "God is dead" philosophers face a primarily Christian problem. For the Jew, God, Israel and Torah are one, hence the absence or denial of God undermines one's existence as a Jew. Theology and peoplehood dwell close together in Jewish life. The mitzvot-directed, this-worldly orientation of Judaism gives all matters of belief and faith a less than central position. Jews have been occupied for a long time with the problem of survival. The time has not yet come when this problem appears antiquarian.

The most serious challenge to Jewish belief is neither this particular constellation of thought nor philosophy and science as disciplines. It is, rather, *scientism,* the elevation of science to the position of arbiter of all human enterprises, the yardstick of thought and action. In this conflict with scientism, Judaism can have the devoted assistance of men in universities who themselves are scientists and yet are rigorously opposed to all dogmatic asseverations, scientific or religious. Scientism has become the pied piper of our younger generation whose hearts and minds we stand in danger of losing unless we can learn to speak to them with words and concepts they can understand, and face them with human tasks to which they can wholly give themselves.

Chapter X

Certain Families Are More Pained Than Others

THERE ARE, AS MIGHT HAVE BEEN EXPECTED, SOME NEWS-
papers and magazines that try to sensationalize the very serious
issue of intermarriage, the assimilation that often follows in
its wake, and the swift decline of the Jewish community in
America. The widely-read *New York* magazine, in a 1990 issue, printed a cover story headline that screamed in big type:
STAR-CROSSED. Under a Star of David, there was a sub-
heading that said, "More Gentiles and Jews are intermarrying—and it's not all chicken soup."

The piece began with a five-year-old kindergarten student
living on New York's Upper West Side, who came home one

day and announced: "I'm Christian and Jewish, and so are Jake and Jess and Katie and Marlow." Traditional Jewish families were undoubtedly taken aback by the child's remarks, which were followed by a 41-year-old Jewish writer declaring his wife, a Presbyterian, who is 39 and a journalist, and he have mostly intermarried friends. "It's the most normal thing in the world," the Jewish writer added—not realizing perhaps that if such an attitude were to prevail, the American Jewish community would disappear very quickly.

And since all small and medium-sized Jewish communities around the world look to the two major Jewish communities, notably America, for guidance, inspiration, know-how, and a host of other forms of assistance, those small communities would soon too begin to shrivel and die off. (The other major Jewish community to which Jews around the world look for leadership is, of course, Israel).

Now, the truth of the matter is that there are Jews who sincerely think that assimilation is the best solution to the age-old problem of the Jews, notably anti-Semitism in its various formulations, and that for them the disappearance of the Jewish people would not be a tragic development. But for most Jews—and for a surprisingly large number of Gentiles—the Jewish people's exiting from the stage of history would be a colossal, catastrophic event that would leave an ugly, permanent scar on humanity.

Certainly there have been ancient peoples who arose, thrived, and then slipped off history's stage. Some left vestiges of their culture, while many did not. But the Jews—that is a different story.

If there had not been a Jewish people struggling for freedom from the oppressive Romans, Jesus might not have arisen when he did to preach his gospels. Christianity might never have been born, nor for that matter Islam. How different the world would be today if Einstein had not lived, or Freud, or even Marx who was baptized a Christian. Would the world still be anguishing from that dread epidemic polio, if Salk and Sabin had not conquered it?

As a speaker mourning the Nazis' massacre of one and a

half-million Jewish children, among the six million, said at a Holocaust memorial: Perhaps among those one and a half-million Jewish children there would have been one who would finally find a cure for the scourge of cancer; perhaps there would have been one whose music would be sung and enjoyed in every section of the world, as has been the music of so many Jewish musicians.

The gradual decline of Jewish identity among Jews in America, and also in Europe, is generally the result of social pressure, or the genuine lack of understanding of what being Jewish means, or a desire to save one's life in a perilous situation.

Ronald Lauder of the Estee Lauder family served as the American ambassador to Austria. He had always been wealthy, privileged and his Jewish identity was probably somewhere on the bottom of his list of priorities. And then along came the shameful episode of the Austrian government and people insisting—no, demanding—that the former secretary-general of the United Nations, Kurt Waldheim, be their next president—notwithstanding overwhelming proof against him that he had been a willing and active Nazi. Lauder protested loudly against Waldheim, so loudly that he apparently was asked to step down as United States ambassador.

Something snapped in Lauder; he turned around and began to do whatever he could to preserve the Jewish identity of the survivors of the Nazi era, small numbers of Jews who had managed to elude capture and massacre and lived mostly in Hungary, Poland and Rumania, and who needed to be taught the basics of the Jewish faith, and the barest outline of Jewish history and culture. Thanks to Lauder, there are now summer camps, religious schools and other educational and cultural facilities for these survivors of the black era of Nazism.

Almost all Jews in America remember the name Henry Morgenthau. He was secretary of the treasury under President Roosevelt, and in 1944 finally succeeded in persuading Roosevelt to establish the War Refugee Board, a rescue agency that succeeded in saving—thanks to the heroic efforts of the Swed-

ish diplomat Raoul Wallenberg and other self-sacrificing people—tens of thousands of Jews, primarily in eastern Europe.

Henry Morgenthau came from a distinguished German-
Jewish family, that traced its origins in America to the mid-
1850s. His father, a successful businessman, served as American ambassador to Turkey and was instrumental early in the
century in helping the beleagured Jewish community in Palestine, at the time a Turkish domain.

After World War II ended, the former secretary of the treasury—who in effect had financed American participation in
the war against the Germans and Japanese—devoted himself
to leading the campaigns of the United Jewish Appeal, and
later the Israel Bond drive. It was obvious that he had been
deeply affected by the Holocaust, and was equally eager to
help put Israel on its feet so that such an obscenity would
never recur.

His grandson, like all the Morgenthaus, had a bare mini-
mum of any kind of Jewish education. But something happened. Some say he met an Orthodox Jewish woman whom he
wished to marry, but she would only agree on condition that
their home be a traditional, kosher, observant home. He
agreed and this scion of the Morgenthau family has adopted a
totally Jewish lifestyle that differs from that of his forbears.

There are other stories circulating in the Jewish community
that make one wonder about the Cassandras. There is a very
successful and wealthy New York businessman whose mother
had died, and for whom he decided to recite the traditional
mourner's prayer, the kaddish. He began to attend the nearest
synagogue, that turned out to be Orthodox with a rabbi who
was one of the most charismatic Jewish preachers-teachers
around. Before long, he altered his whole lifestyle and has become a fully observant, Orthodox Jew committed to the continuity and well-being of the Jewish people.

Another story that has made the rounds deals with the sons
of a multimillionaire Jewish businessman, who had been and
still is a very generous and influential philanthropist. His son
met the daughter of a rabbi, they fell in love, and announced
they would marry and that the son would now become strictly

observant. Soon after, the young man's brother met the young bride's sister, and also fell in love, and they too married and agreed to establish a traditional home. The parents very soon transformed their home into a strictly kosher home so that their sons and daughters-in-law and the girls' parents would feel comfortable when they came to visit.

Nevertheless, the rate of intermarriages nationwide has accelerated dramatically in the last two decades. President Kennedy's daughter married a Jew in her family's church. President Roosevelt's granddaughter married a man called Silberstein. Henry Kissinger's (second) marriage to a Gentile pained many Jews, who knew that his parents were traditional, observant Jews.

There is no Jewish family in the United States that is unaware of a Gentile married to a Jewish relative or friend. In an overwhelming number of cases, parents and grandparents take an "either-or" attitude towards the situation—either I accept intermarriage for my child, or I stand a chance of losing him/her. The vast majority sigh, accept the intermarriage and hope that one day, perhaps when a child is on the way, the Gentile partner will convert to Judaism.

For those families where a son or daughter announces that he/she plans to marry a non-Jew, there is pain and sorrow. It is especially painful for traditional families, where the young person in question was raised to enjoy Jewish life; it is probably even more painful for survivors of the Holocaust, who went through an indescribable hell and who in many cases still bear tattoo marks on their arms.

All of these families, observant and non-observant, newly-arrived in America and those who go back several generations, ask themselves when a child announces plans to intermarry, What can I do? What can I say? Who can help me dissuade my child from leaving the Jewish community? I never thought this would happen to me. . . .

Sometimes parents run to their rabbi, asking for help. And more often than not, he is sympathetic and tries to ease the pain, but he cannot help. One such rabbi I know admitted to a grieving couple that his own nephew had intermarried, and was now virtually cut off from the family.

Synagogues, rabbis, religious teachers, lay leaders, Jewish educators, Jewish organization executives, Jewish newspapers and magazines—everybody deplores the state of affairs that American Jewry finds itself in as the 1990s head for the 21st century. At a meeting of major Jewish leaders, someone suggested that a book be commissioned containing the biographies of highly successful Jews—in a wide range of fields— who have also remained loyal, committed Jews. "They won't read it," someone yells out, cynically. Another says, "How about a subsidized trip for young people to Israel, so they can look around and be inspired?"

"No, that won't work—some of these people have been to Israel, and the others just won't go, even if it's free—you know, they have this cockeyed idea that Israel is a country full of Hasidim, walking around with fur hats."

So what can we do? the leaders ask. We can't just sit back and accept this situation, they say.

Silence fills the room. What is clear to everyone is that each and every young Jewish person contemplating intermarrying is a grown adult, usually an educated individual; he or she feels completely capable of making decisions, and only their immediate families can approach them on so delicate a subject as marriage. The fact that the whole Jewish community is affected is secondary.

Besides, the parents of a youth planning intermarriage, go on, often to themselves, isn't it true that some of the best Jews are converts? So, maybe there will be a conversion, if not before the wedding, afterwards. It's not like in the old days when a father's word was law that a child obeyed.

What many young American Jews fail to understand is the very deep pain that is buried in the collective memory of the Jewish community, especially those Jews past the age of fifty. Whether they wish to or not, large numbers of Jews cannot eject from their minds the pictures of the mass graves, the crematoria, the emaciated skeletons of Jews who survived the

Nazi concentration camps. Nor can they pretend not to see the swastika daubings on synagogues and cemeteries in almost every part of the world, the repeated canards about Jews and Judaism, the refusal of certain politicians to clearly denounce the hatemongers and the inciters to assaults on Jews. There is a feeling of suspicion and distrust in the minds and hearts of Jews vis-a-vis the Gentile world, not only for the centuries of persecution but also for the almost unbelievable fact that blind prejudice against the Jews still continues.

And now along comes a beloved son or daughter, and announces that an intermarriage is planned—with one of them! Of course, this one is different, it is explained. He/she is totally prejudice-free, highly educated, a really fine person. And parents sigh, and wonder, and hope and pray.

They just won't let us be, one mother muses silently. She remembers what happened to her. Back in the thirties, when the Nazis had started their campaign against the Jews of Germany and Austria, before they launched their invasion of Poland, the British government permitted ten thousand Jewish children to enter England, ostensibly until they could be reunited with their parents who were still home, trying to wind up their affairs before their forced emigration.

This mother remembers clearly. She was ten, her older sister sixteen. The two girls were taken by train, first to Paris and then they were to go on to London where various welfare groups would help them find temporary homes. (Many years later, she learned that a similar proposal was made in Congress, to admit some 20,000 Jewish children to the United States, but it was defeated.)

In Paris, the older, 16-year-old sister whispered to her younger sister that she was going to sneak off the train, find a job, earn money and send for their parents. We'll all meet in England, she added, and disappeared. There was no contact between the two sisters for forty years, and when they finally met the older sister revealed what had happened. She managed to get a clerical job, almost on the first day that she was on her own. It was in the office of the Chilean purchasing mission. Her boss was a young Chilean; he fell in love with her, she confided her plans to him, and he convinced her that her parents could not be gotten out of Germany. It was too late. The Nazis' plans for the Jews were advancing too rapidly. Instead, he proposed that they marry, and promised her a good life in Chile and said that her being Jewish did not bother him but if there were any children, he wanted them raised as Catholics. She was a young, terrified, confused teenager, who was now convinced that her idea of rescuing her parents was an impossible dream. Tearfully, she accepted his marriage proposal, and he was as good as his word—they had a comfortable life in Chile, two sons were born to them, both boys were raised as Catholics, and she herself—embittered by the certain loss of her parents and by the turn of events in her life—turned away from Judaism, from God, from all religion.

She made a few feeble efforts to find her sister in England during and after the war, failed and then gave it up. What she did not know was that her sister became a nurse, volunteered to help Holocaust survivors who were arriving in Palestine, met an American volunteer and soon they were married and settled in the United States. It was only through the determined efforts of her husband that the two sisters finally met, decades later.

When they were reunited, the younger sister realized very quickly that her older sister was really no longer Jewish. She disdained all religion, and rejected any mention of Jewish tradition or observance. As the younger sister said to her husband, when they were alone, she too is a victim of Hitler, even after all these years.

And now, this younger sister, a woman in her sixties, hears her son announce that he has fallen in love with a Christian girl, and they plan to marry. Try as she might, her tears cannot be stopped.

Stuart Matlins, formerly a management consultant who lived and worked on the fast track in Manhattan, gave it all up to live a more peaceful and serene life in Vermont. He drifted into the somewhat esoteric field of Jewish book publishing. He explains: "I came to understand how much spiritual hunger there is out there, how many Jews think the synagogue is not relevant to them and their lives. But—the problem is not with Judaism, it's with their knowledge of what Judaism is all about. I wanted to reach out to our brothers and sisters who think Judaism has no meaning for them."

In the books that his company produces, Matlins explains, "We try to convey the diversity of Jewish views. We speak with many voices. One goal is to unite Jews by showing the diversity of our experience. Judaism has beauty, (there is) beauty in our language, our culture, our soul."

As a Jewish book publisher, Matlins says, we are "trying to attract, educate, engage and spiritually inspire. We are trying to create an inspirational literature that allows creative Jewish minds to be heard, and that shows the relevance of Judaism to everyday life as we enter the twenty-first century." Matlins says that the name of his company, Jewish Lights, is meant to communicate to "the Gentile world the concept that Jews are a light unto the nations."

American Jews were startled and saddened to learn from a new study that 20 per cent of all Americans do not believe that the Holocaust ever took place. That adds up to 50 million people in the United States. Many thought to themselves: First, they kill and torture us, and now—only 50 years later—a new generation says, No, it never even happened!

What can we do? Drag 50,000,000 people in America into the Holocaust museum in Washington, and show them?

Besides, we Jews really want to stop thinking about the Holocaust, we want to get on with our lives, we want to share our children's and grandchildren's joys and achievements. On the other hand, how can we just walk away from this unbelievable fact—50 million Americans don't even believe it happened! That is the worst crime of all! Worse even than the actual massacres!

The name Louis Brandeis, for most Jews, calls up the picture of a lanky silver-haired member of the United States Supreme Court, the first Jew ever to serve on that august body.

He was known in his earlier years as the "People's Attorney," a fighter for justice—for women, for children who were put to work at very early ages, for working people who had no one to defend them against big business and big corporations. Many of the laws that were enacted in the early years of the twentieth century for the benefit of workers, women and children came about as the result of Brandeis' persistent efforts. He simply could not allow unjust situations to continue, and fought them in the courts, and later as a justice of the Supreme Court.

What is interesting about Brandeis is the evolution of his Jewish identity. He was born in Louisville, Kentucky, during the Civil War. His parents had fled the Bohemia region of central Europe because of anti-Jewish outbreaks, and apparently decided to start a whole new life in the New World—without any religion whatsoever. However, Brandeis' mother's brother held fast to Jewish tradition and observance, and became not only a respected lawyer but also an early leader in Jewish scholarly and religious circles.

Louis Brandeis never had a bar mitzvah. A brilliant student in his home town, he was admitted to Harvard where he achieved record-breaking marks. He knew he had been born Jewish, but it meant little if anything to him. He and a distant cousin were married not by a rabbi but by a leader of the new Ethical Culture movement. By the time he was fifty, Brandeis had achieved great success in his profession and in his private life. He and his wife were raising two daughters and sent them to good schools. Everything seemed to be on an even keel, but that was only on the surface.

Certain events had taken place that had begun to touch him. In 1881 there were brutal pogroms against defenseless Jews in Russia; hundreds died and many thousands sought to escape to America. A man called Theodor Herzl, a Hungarian Jewish journalist, who had witnessed the trial of Captain Alfred Dreyfus, the French Jewish officer convicted of treason on trumped up charges, reacted by producing a booklet called "The Jewish State," calling for the re-creation of ancient Israel. The pogroms, the Dreyfus trial, his later exoneration and the mob's continuing cries of "Death to the Jews," and Herzl's successful efforts to organize a mass movement to bring the Jews back to their ancient homeland in Palestine—all of this stirred something in Brandeis. He began to donate more and more funds to Jewish causes, but the one single experience that transformed him into an active, committed Jew took place in New York. Brandeis had been asked to act as arbitrator between the workers and the bosses in the largely Jewish garment industry. A bitter strike had been going on for months, and both sides conceded that they no longer knew how to end it.

For the first time in his life, Brandeis came up against east European Jews—Orthodox, Bible-quoting Jews who were proud of their heritage, disdained those who hid their Jewish background, and felt they could live in America openly and freely as Jews who were the proud possessors of a culture of more than three thousand years.

The only Jews Brandeis had known before were Germanic, from central Europe, who seemed often to waver between remaining Jewish or marrying a Gentile and abandoning the Jewish community. It was an eye-opening experience for Brandeis; he felt that these east European Jews were the direct descendants of the biblical prophets, who were not embarrassed to speak of ideals, social justice, fair play—subjects that Brandeis always felt himself drawn to.

Thus, for the second half of his life, Brandeis became a new kind of Jew—new for him. When the nascent Zionist movement in America needed a strong, respected American Jew to lead it, he accepted the offer of the presidency and threw himself into speaking, writing, and organizing. His prestige and enthusiasm persuaded thousands of American Jews to extend their support to the early efforts to rebuild the ancient Jewish homeland in Palestine.

There can be little doubt that thousands of American Jews looked to Brandeis for guidance and inspiration, and he never failed them. During all his years as a Supreme Court justice, he continued to support many Zionist programs. When he was at an advanced age he made his one and only trip to Palestine, met the kibbutz colonists, traveled up and down the country, sensing the ancient history of the Jews and confident that one day soon new history would be written there. The trip to Palestine invigorated his spirit, he often said. Whether he regretted having been detached from the Jewish people in the first fifty years of his life he never said.

He certainly would have been proud to know that there is today a Jewish sponsored university named for him; there is a kibbutz in Israel bearing his name; and numerous chapters of Jewish and Zionist organizations are named for him. One of his two daughters became an active leader of Hadassah, a fact that would certainly have pleased him.

There is a Yiddish expression that claims that there exists in every Jew—no matter how assimilated, no matter how distant from the Jewish community—something called *dos pintele yid*. Translated, this means the "little Jewish dot." In Brandeis' case, the dot surfaced, grew and helped make him one of the great figures in American Jewish history.

Popeye—remember him?

This popular cartoon character used to say, while bulging his muscles:

> I am what I am
> 'cause that's what I am,
> I'm Popeye the sailor man.

To me that means simply that each person must be true to himself, and must at all times be himself. A Jew born into a great tradition should enjoy it, live it, learn it, share it, grow with it. Squelching it or hiding it sounds like a formula for inner turmoil. One should come to feel that being Jewish is both a lucky happenstance, and an opportunity to serve humanity.

Chapter XI

Do All Jewish Parents Really Educate Children in Judaism?

BEING JEWISH—TRULY JEWISH—MEANS ADHERING TO A year-round, daily way of life that includes virtually every facet of a person's life. It does not mean that a Jew needs to spend all of his waking time praying, nor does it mean that a Jew should devote all his time to Jewish studies—although there are some Jews who do devote themselves to full-time prayer or full-time study.

It means that Judaism, or being Jewish, is a way of life that touches on practically every aspect of life, from the mundane to the spiritual, and every contact that Jewishness brings to bear on an individual is meant to make that person more ethical, more serene, more healthy in mind and in body, and more of an active, contributing member of a society that is, very slowly admittedly, inching along toward a better, more peaceful, more friendly world.

Many Jewish parents in the '90s, and in the decades before, complained to whoever would listen that their children were alienated from Judaism; they generally added that they, the parents, had given them "everything," including everything that "we did not have when we were their age." Unfortunately, many of these well-meaning parents, usually those who were affiliated with Conservative or Reform synagogues more so than with Orthodox houses of worship, or those who were unaffiliated, did not themselves understand the essence of Judaism, and what they had been trying to pass on to their children all too often was a watered down, uninformed and often childish version of Jewish life—to children who were usually sophisticated college graduates who had been exposed for a number of years to the best of western civilization, except, of course, to Judaism courses.

Thus, when an adult child was visiting in the home of the parents, he/she would frequently go through the motions of a Passover seder service, or joining the parents in synagogue for the briefest amount of time possible on the High Holy Days— and then detach themselves for the rest of the year from something they thought to be "old-fashioned" or "suitable for the old folks."

In effect the chasm that develops between growing, maturing children and their parents was made even wider and deeper by the issue of Judaism. Parents simply had not succeeded in explaining to their children the value system entailed in Judaism; sometimes, the more they tried to define the essence of being Jewish, the more their children decided that Jewishness was like a hobby, something to be picked up in one's spare time, to help while away a few hours. More importantly, most Jewish parents were themselves unwilling to dedicate their own free time to serious Jewish study, or Sabbath synagogue attendance, or traditional Sabbath and holiday observance, or taking on responsibility for aiding a Jewish institution or charity—so why should their children do so?

Ironically, there has been a growing phenomenon of Jewish families—anxious that their children succeed in life and choose a suitable profession as their life's work—who have fought against giving their children any kind of environment that might be interpreted as "too Jewish." Instead of sending their children to a good Jewish all-day school in the neighborhood, they chose to send them to a well-known private school with absolutely no Jewish connections whatsoever, so that when the time comes for applying to an Ivy League university, it would look good on their application. It stands to reason that a Jewish teenager who thus becomes alienated from close contact with Jewish life will quickly conclude that Judaism or being a Jew is a rather unimportant part of one's background. In the course of time that young person will come to regard his being a Jew as of no value or importance, making him/her a very likely candidate for an intermarriage a few years down the road.

Jewish parents confronted with the way they are raising their children will explain that they are more "universal" in their outlook on life, and that Judaism is really too "narrow" for them. It becomes their excuse for not teaching their children the basics of being Jewish, and in effect prepares that youngster for the next step—intermarriage and assimilation.

Often such parents will declare in their own defense, "Well, if he would have wanted to have a bar mitzvah or take advanced Jewish studies," we would not have stood in his way. There is no doubt they believe what they say, but what they fail to realize is young people still in their teens are still malleable; they swiftly sense that despite what their parents might say, the Jewish aspect of their family's life is really of no significance. When they were small, these youths may very well muse, *the parents insisted that they brush their teeth every day, and wear a sweater on a cold day, and never did they inculcate any Jewish lessons in us. So—it can't be very important, can it?*

The tragic truth is that great numbers of Jewish youths are being raised in homes where Judaism is an occasional visitor, not a permanent resident. It's all well and good to proclaim universalism as the goal of all ethical people—but that does not mean ignoring one's own religious-cultural-historic roots. Quite the contrary, a genuine knowledge and understanding of one's heritage will enable a committed Jew to join in mankind's quest for a worldwide peaceful future. Experience has proven that ignorance of one's background, or totally ignoring one's roots, all too often leads a young person to become a candidate for a brain-washing cult. The young Jews who allow themselves to be swept into cults seem to be seeking for a way of life in which they can be told what to do, from morning till night. In Judaism, there is also a system of precepts that is offered to a young person, encompassing one's whole life, but—*and here is the crucial difference*—it is not coercive, one can accept or reject, or accept in part. The young Jews caught up in the cults have no knowledge of a way of life that Judaism offers, and thus become instant prey for cults and their gurus.

There also exists in the minds of many American Jews in the '90s the idea that knowledge of Judaism is not really as important as knowledge of the world around us. If you tell these people that the great Maimonides studied and gratefully acknowledged the work of Aristotle, or that Rabbi Joseph Soloveichik, the preeminent talmudist of the 20th century, acknowledged his debt to the Protestant theologian Kirkegaard, they remain unimpressed. Physics, mathematics, chemistry, electronics—these are what our children should be studying and mastering—for their own personal, professional development, and also for the good of society, they say. For these Jews, generally Jewishly illiterate, Judaism is a secondary or even tertiary topic.

One man who would totally disagree is a distinguished physicist whose reputation has already spread around the world. His name is Herman Branover, and he is one of hundreds of thousands of Jews who have emigrated from the former Soviet Union to Israel. Until he was in his thirties, Branover—like all Soviet citizens—was not allowed to study the Bible, or study Hebrew, or observe any religious practice. Then something happened: he began to pick up smatterings of his Jewish roots. Secretly, he studied Bible, and soon realized that he had been thirsty for his unknown Jewishness all his life. In the course of time he emigrated to Israel, adopted a very Orthodox lifestyle, and today continues his advanced work as a physicist-researcher—some of it on contract with the United States Navy for developing new sources of electric power. Ever since the arrival in Israel of very large numbers of Russian immigrants—many of them scientists—Branover has also been actively trying to ease their absorption into Israeli life, and at the same time he is seeking to teach his fellow Russian emigres the basics of Judaism which, he often says, gave him a new lease on life.

There are numerous cases of American Jews who hid their Jewishness practically all their lives, and not until they were in their last years did they choose to rejoin their people, and try to make amends.

One of the stories is of the well-known engineer-industrialist, Gerard Swope, the grandson of a rabbi, who changed his name and told no one for more than a half-century that he had been born Gershom Schwab in St. Louis, and that at an early age he made up his mind to become an electrical engineer—a new field that was just beginning to develop. Young Gershom knew that Jews in the early 1920s were not being accepted by America's leading universities, including the prestigious Massachusetts Institute of Technology, where he wished to study.

Now known as Gerard Swope, the young man applied to MIT and was accepted. He was an outstanding student, and when he graduated was launched on an almost meteoric rise to success. In not too many years he became the chief executive officer of General Electric, and helped it grow into one of the world's leading corporations.

Meanwhile, he got married to a non-Jewish woman, and the Swopes soon had two children. All was well, but deep in Swope there lay this secret knowledge that he was a Jew, and that his successful life was built on a false premise. But as head of GE, Swope had little time for meditating too much about his inner problem. When America entered World War II after Pearl Harbor, General Electric, under Swope's direction, played a vital role in helping to assure victory for the western powers and defeat for the Nazis.

Swope was always a sensitive man, and during the '30s and early '40s, the pictures of the concentration camps' victims sickened him. The subsequent reports of the total, deliberate destruction of six million European Jews appalled him. Then, three years later, the State of Israel proclaimed its independence, and Swope could rejoice, but this too he did in secret. His wife had begun to ail and he was busy caring for her, never expecting that she would pre-decease him. She died soon after, and he found himself a lonely, lost man.

He had become a multimillionaire from his position at GE, and he now began to think of what to do with his funds. The first thing he did was make financial provision for his children. And then he made a trip to Israel, in the early '50s, quietly, without fanfare. He told a friend later he wished to look around, to see for himself the survivors of the Holocaust and to look at what had been achieved in ancient Palestine by the young generation of pioneers.

Apparently his visit made a strong impression on him. He saw the survivors, he saw the kibbutzim, the agricultural settlements, he saw the young Israeli soldiers; he was moved and decided to do something lasting for Israel. In the meantime, no one knew that Gerard Swope was Jewish; they only knew that the retired head of GE was on a private visit to Israel.

As a former MIT student and subsequent alumnus and supporter, Swope went to see Israel's then small engineering university, the Technion, located in Haifa. He was ushered around to classes, laboratories, met some of the professors—and made up his mind. While in Israel he had made no commitments.

Upon his return to America, he got in touch with one of the leaders of the American Technion Society, a volunteer group that sought to provide aid to the Haifa institution. This individual, to Swope's surprise, was a man senior to him in years, an attorney wise in the ways of the world. He told Swope that he himself, as an officer in the U.S. Army in World War I had met and fallen in love with and married a German woman, who had converted to Judaism and who was herself now a very active supporter of various groups aiding Israel. Slowly, the words poured out of Swope. For fifty years he had not said a word, but now he was "confessing"—he was a Jew, and he wished to leave a bequest that would help Israel and the Technion, and that perhaps would ease the decades-old pain in his heart. The sum, he added, was not small—it was approximately $10 million.

A few years later, Swope died. He had stipulated that he wanted nothing in Israel named for him, but preferred that the fund he was bequeathing become a permanent source of income for scholarships, for faculty aid, for research.

Technion today—known as the MIT of Israel—has this perpetual fund which enables many students and professors to learn and to teach, and to help advance science and technology not only in Israel but also in all peace-loving countries. It is rated as one of the world's finest such universities—partly because one man—albeit late in life—had regained his Jewish identity and made amends for hiding his Jewish roots.

It is sad when a young person raised in a non-observant, unaffiliated Jewish home opts to break away from his Jewish roots; it is also sad when that home is essentially not a religiously-committed home but one where the parents believe that just because they are active in Hadassah or are large donors to the United Jewish Appeal, or to the local synagogue, that that is enough to keep their children actively committed to the Jewish community, just like the parents.

Unfortunately, it doesn't work that way. Many, many Jewish parents who are now in their 50s or 60s grew up remembering the frightening years of Nazi ascendancy in the world; they always bear in the back of their minds the horror of the Holocaust; and they possess a deeply emotional attachment to Israel as the one sure place on earth where Jews in peril can flee and be saved from whatever new threat looms over the horizon. The children, on the other hand, do not remember the

Holocaust—they only read about it; they were born after Israel was established, and for them Israel has always been there, and it is a country like many others, although it is true that it is the only country in the world that has a Jewish majority. The two generations' attitudes towards Judaism differ radically. It is important that the older generation understands this, and in talking to their children keeps this factor in mind.

Another vexing problem that surfaces in some younger Jews involves those who have had a substantial Jewish education, and who came from homes where Jewishness and Judaism appeared to be an essential part of their daily lives. What sometimes happens is that the parents—despite the fact that they went through all the rituals of Judaism—did not, in their children's estimation, lead ethical, sincere lives in keeping with the noblest ideals of Judaism. The educated, sophisticated children of such families either looked away, or turned against their parents for what they perceived to be hypocrisy—creating a wedge between the generations that often did not heal for many years.

Then there is another kind of religious environment established by parents who, when being asked questions by their children about basic precepts or practices, had the unfortunate habit of answering by saying, "Don't ask! That's what the Torah says—do it!" In the vast majority of cases, such a response is almost guaranteed to turn young Jews completely off. It may be acceptable for a three-year-old, but certainly not for an intelligent, questing, questioning, eighteen-year-old. Parents must learn to explain the logical reasons for a religious law, or custom, or admit they do not know and suggest that the rabbi be asked.

What is urgently important for parents to convey to their adult children—if they do not wish to see intermarriage and assimilation grow—is that Judaism's goal is to assure that Jews do not forget God. As the Jewish prayerbook states plainly, the Jewish people's role in the world was and is "to perfect the world under the rule of God." And as a reminder of this concept, one must remember the pithy comment of that great scholar and theologian, Rabbi Abraham Joshua Heschel:

"The Jewish people is (like) a messenger who forgot the message."

In the 1990s the threat of intermarriage, assimilation and the steady disappearance of large numbers of Jews from the American Jewish community has become the principal challenge confronting the community's leaders. The ultra-Orthodox Jews still maintain that self-isolation and self-ghettoization in order to reduce the possibilities of contact between young Jews and young Christians is the best answer to this problem; however, the overwhelming majority of American Jews reject it. We wish to be part and parcel of the American community, to work with and mix with all people, and somehow to find a solution to this problem.

Short of full-scale immigration to Israel, many American Jewish and Israeli leaders are recommending that all Jews, young and not-so-young, spend a limited amount of time in Israel in order to expose them to an environment in which Jews are the majority. It is a fact that almost all young Jews who spend a summer visiting Israel, or a semester at an Israeli school of higher learning, or as volunteers working on a communal farm, return full of enthusiasm and praise for Israel, and new understanding of themselves as Jews. According to Jewish educators, both those in America and those in Israel, a Jewish teenager who spends a year in Israel during his high school period will remain forever committed to remaining Jewish. And adults who can take off a year from their jobs and bring along their families, these same educators maintain, will also be making one of the wisest investments of their lives—a year in Israel, for young and old, absorbing the spirit of the country, the easy Jewishness that flows just from being the majority, the study of Hebrew, Bible and Jewish culture and religion—all these steps will ensure the continuity of the Jewish community in the United States, and will become a powerful weapon against intermarriage.

Whether or not these steps can be or will be taken remains to be seen. One of the national leaders of American Jewry, Mrs. Shoshanah Cardin, addressing what amounted to an emergency gathering dealing with the issue of intermarriage, said late in 1992 that "Jewish identity and continuity are our driving force and key words . . . it is our new primacy."

Speaking at the same gathering, Professor Leonard Fein stressed that "we must explain to the next generation of American Jews . . . in a compelling way . . . what it is that warrants the survival of Judaism." Robert Lipton, president of the American Jewish Congress, who voiced doubts that Jewish education alone can slow the rate of intermarriage and assimilation, which he described as a "powerful force," noted that was what urgently needed was "great inspiration—that only Israel is capable of providing in the dimensions required to make a real difference in American Jewish life."

Historians have noted that in virtually every generation some Jews have chosen to convert to the majority religion and meld into the mainstream. They did this because they felt it was the quickest and easiest way to achieve economic, social or political success, or sometimes out of genuine conviction, and sometimes, of course, because in certain situations not to do so was tantamount to asking for an early death. The late Gerson Cohen, chancellor of the Jewish Theological Seminary in New York and a respected historian, always insisted that there was a better way—to meet the situation head-on and allow the fundamental precepts of Judaism to prevail.

There were historical periods when the Hebrew language was not used, and what Jews did use was Aramaic or Greek, something that was feared would lead to the immediate disappearance of the Jewish community, Cohen noted. The importance of keeping one's Jewish names was also ignored during certain historic periods, but what happened was that Jews at first took on these foreign names, and then creatively Hebraized them. Thus, for example, some of the names that we know today as distinctly Jewish names—Moses, Aaron, Phinehas—started out as Egyptian names.

What Dr. Cohen was saying was that what may at first appear to be a step toward assimilation and disappearance may also, because of Jewish creativity, be turned around and become absorbed into Jewish life and culture. As he said in a talk some years ago, "A frank appraisal of the periods of great Jewish creativity will indicate that not only did a certain amount of assimilation and acculturation *not* impede Jewish continuity and creativity but that in a profound sense this assimilation or acculturation was even a stimulus to original thinking and expression and, consequently, a source of renewed vitality.

"To a considerable degree," Cohen continued, "the Jews survived as a vital group and as a pulsating culture because they changed their names, their language, their clothing and with them some of their patterns of thought and expression. . . .There are two ways of meeting the problem of assimilation. The first is withdrawal and fossilization. . . . There always was an alternative approach of taking the bull by the horns, as it were, and utilizing the inevitable inroads of assimilation as channels of new sources of vitality. . . . Assimilation bears within it a certain seminal power which serves as a challenge and a goad to renewed creativity."

Not everyone will agree with Dr. Cohen's assessment, but it is a view that has a limited number of followers in the United States.

Another historian, the late Lucy Davidowicz, recalls in her book *The Jewish Presence* that in 1942—after the Nazis had crushed Poland, France and several smaller countries, and had steamrollered their way into the Soviet Union—Jews trapped in the Vilna Ghetto were having an intellectual discussion. Their subject was "Jewish identity," something most of them had never given any thought to up to that moment. The Jewish intellectuals looked about them in the ghetto, and saw that they were confined together with all sorts of people called Jews, with whom they seemed to have very little in common. They talked around the subject, and reached no conclusion.

Nevertheless, Davidowicz writes,

There is unambiguous criteria in Jewish law . . . which define who is a Jew, but no such clarity prevails as to *what* is a Jew in the modern world. You may be a Jew only in the sense that you were born to Jewish parents. You may be a Jew because you were raised as one, in a family informed by Jewish tradition and molded by Jewish history. You may be a Jew if you were educated to be one, parents and teachers having transmitted a body of Jewish knowledge and a system of Jewish beliefs. You may be a Jew because your family reared you to observe Jewish law and because the milieu in which you choose to live observes that law and enforces its conduct. You may be a Jew by speaking Yiddish, by proclaiming you love Yiddish, even by denying you know Yiddish. You may be a Jew just by not being a Christian or a pagan. Or you may be a Jew only by living among Jews. You may be a Jew only by being marginal, poised between two cultures, never quite at home in either. Or your Jewishness may be evident only in a stamp of restlessness, a cast of skepticism, an affinity for irony. Or by the contempt you inflict on yourself and the destructiveness you discharge on others. You may be a Jew in your own eyes, in the eyes of other Jews, or only in the eyes of non-Jews. You may curse the day you were born a Jew or celebrate your being one.

What makes one a Jew? Identity, as Erik H. Erikson has told us, has its first locus in "the core of the individual and yet also in the core of his communal culture." Each person's individuality is determined by his unique psyche developed in mutual interaction with his social milieu, his culture. That culture, in turn, is shaped by history. The intersection of individuality, culture and history becomes the crucible where selfhood is born.

With mother's milk the child imbibes the values and traditions of his group and culture. . . . Modern Jewish mothers no longer sing Yiddish lullabies, but like mothers in all cultures, classes and societies, they rear their babies into awareness that the world is divided into camps: We and They."

Chapter XII

Did Assimilation Take Over for Ambition?

IN HIS HIGHLY RECOMMENDED BOOK, *THIS IS MY GOD,* THE novelist Herman Wouk—who is an observant, committed and knowledgeable Jew—touches on the problem of assimilation. When he was seventeen, he writes, a fraternity brother said to him, "The best thing we can do is intermarry and disappear."

He reacted, he writes: "It was the first time I had heard the slogan of assimilation spoken loud and clear. It froze me. I peered at him, wondering whether he could be serious. He was. The assimilators are always quite serious, though some Jews find their state of mind unimaginable."

Wouk writes:

Assimilation is, and for the longest time has been, a main party of dissent in Jewry. It does not seem a party, because in its nature it has no organization, no temples, no schools, and no books of doctrine. But in periods of freedom like the present—and there have been several such interludes in our history—it sometimes wins half of the Jews, and occasionally more than half.

To call the assimilators turncoats, weaklings, traitors, breakers of the faith, is to substitute abuse for the effort to think. Assimilation is not only a popular way, it has weighty logic on its side. The real surprise is that the Jews have not wholly evaporated in one of these times of tolerance. What, to be given the chance to lay down the burden of ostracism and disappear among the billions of mankind, and not take advantage of it with a rush and a cheer? Where is the sense—in view of the sombre history of the Jews—in behaving any other way?

With all that, the assimilator seldom states his position in the cold blood of my fraternity brother. Nor does he, as a rule, plot a course of vanishing. He allows it to happen. This is achieved simply by doing nothing about being Jewish. Three or four generations, and the family ceases to count as Jews, unless bloodthirsty lunatics like the Nazis start up a grandfather hunt. Remaining Jewish in a free society takes work. If the work goes undone, Jewishness dims and dies. It is the exceptional assimilator who tries to speed the death by such devices as changing his name and obscuring or denying his background.

Assimilation, like frostbite, begins at the extremities of Jewry. Settlements far from centers of the community almost always fade away fast. In the social body it is the wealthiest and the poorest, the best educated and the least educated, the brightest and the dullest, who tend to go first. Ignorance and low intelligence cause loss of grip on the faith. Carried along in the ghetto by the current around them, the ill-informed and the incapable drift into non-observance when cut loose, and into oblivion. Poverty drives people to suspend observance, and grinds away their identity. At the other extreme the rich and the gifted make their way swiftly into the non-Jewish world. Judaism being an encumbrance on the way, they tend to drop it. It is in the middle that Jewish identity persists longest, whether as Zionism, orthodoxy or religious dissent.

Yet here too assimilation at last takes hold. When professors and governors, movie stars and millionaires, writers and judges openly give up their Jewish ties and ways—these in America, and their equivalents in Germany, Spain, Morocco, Rome and Babylon in other days—the wonder is that anybody at all remains behind to carry on the faith. Yet a remnant always does, and Judaism in time renews itself with the greatest struggles—if only to produce, in the next age of tolerance, another wave of gifted assimilators. It is even argued that this is the true mission of the Jews, the secret of the Messiah symbol—that they must go on relinquishing to the world St. Pauls, Spinozas, Freuds, Disraelis. It is a fetching idea. One weakness of it is that if assimilation ever won a round of history, the milieu and the human strain that produce such luminaries would disappear and the world would see no more of them.

The loss of these intelligences in the van of a new assimilation surge is each time foredoomed. Quickest to see the conflicts of the old way and the new, they are the first to decide that Judaism is dated. They find in their mastery of the new life, in the welcome granted to their talents, a whole answer to existence. They create a climate in which assimilation becomes first a smart, then an ordinary course. Masses of plain people follow them without the compensations of high achievement, simply because it is always easier not to be Jewish, once the communion weakens.

The odd thing is that this momentous rejection by the able few is almost never a well-considered act. Often they are born of parents already adrift, so that they never get a chance to know Judaism. Or if they find a received form of it in their homes, it loses out swiftly to the interests generated by their special talents. By the age of fifteen they have swept into a life, and a state of mind, which exclude forever an adult estimate of their Jewish identity. It is a freakish occurrence when—as with Heine—a man of genius has second thoughts about assimilation, reopens the case with all his energies, and reverses the verdict. And such a rare event comes too late, both for the man and for the people who have followed him.

A well-known and successful individual who resides in New York was born on the Lower East Side, to the poorest of the poor. Until he entered public school at age six he spoke only Yiddish. Slowly, he learned; ambition to better his station in life thrust him ever forward. He threw off his humble origins, and with them all vestiges of his Jewish background. Somehow, he equated grinding poverty with Judaism. In the course of time he changed his name. His speech gave the impression that he had studied at one of the most prestigious of America's Ivy League colleges, which he had not. He married a Jewish woman, and together they created a home and a family in the suburbs that was religiously, Jewishly sterile. None of their three children attended religious school, nor did they celebrate a bar or bat mitzvah. On a major Jewish holiday, when it would have been unseemly for this individual to be seen at work as usual, he usually took his family on an excursion out-of-town. He was a good father, a good husband, a good neighbor, and a Jew adrift in a sea of assimilation.

One daughter married a Catholic young man of Polish parentage. His son married a Presbyterian young woman, whose ancestry was English. And the other daughter met, fell in love with and eventually married a strictly observant Jewish physician. The young doctor patiently went about teaching his wife about Judaism—the customs, the rules, the meanings of various traditions, the lifestyle of a modern Orthodox Jewish family.

The children of the religious couple attend a Jewish day school. Their cousins are being raised with no faith, and will probably in the course of the years drift into marriage with Christians. Sometimes, the grandfather, in the privacy of his home, late at night when his wife is asleep, berates himself for raising his children the way he did. From a bottom drawer of his desk he removes a prayerbook, dons a yarmulke and repeats some of the prayers that he knew so well as a child.

He has attended the circumcision ceremony of his younger daughter's son and the baptism ceremony for his son's child. In his heart of hearts he feels ill at ease; he wonders if there is anything he can do, at this late date.

From the late 1800s through the 1900s, Jews were exposed to unparalleled upheavals. In the latter part of the nineteenth century, most Jews lived in eastern Europe. Pogroms—state-sponsored assaults on defenseless Jewish communities—characterized the condition of the Jews in the small hamlets and villages during the 1880s and 1890s. As a result, hundreds of thousands of Russian, Polish and Rumanian Jews fled, mostly to America, while others found haven in England, Canada, Argentina and a minuscule number in Turkish-controlled Palestine. Families were separated, often for many decades.

The refugees in western Europe and North America, and in Argentina, found work almost immediately. In Palestine, life was far more difficult, and some of the refugees picked themselves up again and moved on to the United States and Canada.

In France a trumped-up case against a Jewish officer, Captain Dreyfus, revealed the deep hatred for Jews that the French people bore; even after Dreyfus' exoneration and restoration to his military position, calls for "death to the Jews" continued. One result of the Dreyfus trial was the transformation of a young Austrian Jewish journalist, Theodor Herzl, from an assimilating Jew into a fiery fighter for Jewish political rights. His reaction to the trial was to launch the world Zionist movement.

The ideal of the restoration of the old-new Land of Israel gradually caught on; from Russia, young idealistic Jews sought to be rid of pogroms and anti-Semitism once and for all, and set out on foot to reach Palestine and begin the task of rebuilding a country that had been almost abandoned for two millenia. In the western countries, the newly-arrived refugees were deeply grateful to find that they lived in democratic countries where they enjoyed equal rights with all other citizens. They studied the customs and language of the country in which they lived, became naturalized citizens, and raised a generation of native-born children in an environment of freedom. World War I was a difficult time, when Jews in the western armies fought against Jews in the German and Austrian armies; the revolution that swept Russia in the 1917–1919 period brought new waves of Jewish escapees to the western world and to Palestine.

The decade of the 1920s, which should have been a time of peace, ended disastrously with the 1929 stock market crash, which brought severe suffering to millions of people, including most Jews who were still struggling to find a place for themselves. This decade in turn was followed by the rise of Hitlerism in the early 1930s, and the threat that this development posed for all Jews around the world.

Pogroms, mass dislocations, war, depression, Nazism—it is a wonder that vast numbers of Jews did not surrender their Jewish identity, and convert to Christianity. To be a Jew seemed to be a thing of peril; but the Jews of that era did not convert and abandon Judaism.

Instead, they united and as much as they could they fought back. When the Nazis in 1933 burned all the Jewish books they could get their hands on in bonfires throughout Germany, the American Jewish community responded by establishing a new cultural agency, the Jewish Book Council, to encourage the writing and publishing of Jewish books. When it became apparent that the worst was yet to come as the Nazis strengthened their position, the American Jews established the United Jewish Appeal, to provide for Jewish refugees reaching the United States, for displaced Jews living in transit centers in European and Asian countries, and for aid to the nascent agricultural communes in Palestine which would soon be admitting larger numbers of Jewish escapees.

The spread of Nazi propaganda against Jews in the United States stimulated the creation of special organizations to fight back by all means possible, including infiltrating some pro-Nazi groups.

Jews, it seemed in those days, were under constant attack. Their response was to unite, and fight back, and simultaneously aid fellow Jews in need. There was never any talk of assimilation and disappearance. Jews felt that they were innocent of any wrongdoing, they believed that they had brought the world many centuries of invaluable contributions, and that the Jewish heritage was eminently worth defending and fighting for. In that period, when a Jew married a Christian— a rare event—the Christian almost always chose to convert to Judaism.

In ancient days, the word assimilation as it was applied to the people of Israel had a very different meaning from what it generally means today. In the reigns of the great kings, David and Solomon, assimilation was seen as a natural way of increasing the strength of the Israelites. Israel assimilated into itself various tribes, offering them a monotheistic faith; the *Encyclopedia Judaica* notes that there were times when conquering Israelite armies compelled their defeated enemies to accept Judaism and become new members of the Israelite nation.

In modern times, of course, the word has a totally different connotation: Jews, always a minority (until the establishment of Israel), considered assimilating into the larger mainstream of people among whom they live as a method of avoiding future attacks and discrimination, and as a way to improve their economic and social opportunities.

The pendulum of history and assimilation swung in two very different directions through the ages. For example, the Phoenician people, who lived along the sea in what is today Israel (and to a lesser extent also in what is today southern Lebanon), were fully assimilated into the Israelite mainstream. On the other hand, in Alexandria, which was a major Greek cultural center where there was a large, active Jewish community, virtually all the Jews over the course of time were assimilated into the population.

When the Nazis came to power in Germany in 1933, a German Jew by the name of Ernst Toller was in turmoil. He had always thought of himself as a patriotic German, whose Jewishness was secondary. But a year after the Nazis began their anti-Semitic campaigns that eventually led to the Holocaust, Toller wrote:

> I thought of my terrible joy when I realized nobody recognized me for a Jew . . . of my passionate longing to prove I was a real German by offering my life to my country . . . of my writing to the authorities to say they could strike my name from the list of the Jewish community. Had it all been for nothing? Had it all been wrong? Didn't I love Germany with all my heart? . . . But wasn't I also a Jew? A member of that great race that for centu-

ries had been persecuted, harried, martyred and slain? Whose prophets called on the world for righteousness, who exalted the wretched and the poor, then and for all time? A race who never bowed their heads to their persecutors, who preferred death to dishonor? I had denied my own mother and I was ashamed . . . How much of me was German, and how much Jewish? Pride and love are not the same thing . . . If I were asked where I belong, I would answer: A Jewish mother had borne me, Germany nourished me, Europe formed me, my home was the earth, and the world my fatherland.

During the colonial period in the United States, there were only about two thousand Jews living in the country. Most of them were Sephardic, the descendants of those Sephardic Jews expelled from Spain and Portugal in the late fifteenth century who had lived in Holland, Poland, England, Brazil and Italy. There were far more men that women, and steadily the rate of intermarriage between Jews and Christians grew. Almost none of the descendants of those early Jewish settlers in America have remained Jewish.

However, in the wake of the Holocaust and following the establishment of Israel in 1948, there was very little inclination on the part of American Jews to intermarry and assimilate. Besides, as the *Encyclopedia Judaica* notes, after World War II, "American society became more open to Jews than any country has ever been throughout the whole history of the Diaspora. . . . The Holocaust and the creation of the State of Israel caused many Jews to reaffirm their Jewish identity. The rapid economic rise of the bulk of the American Jewish community into the middle and upper middle classes during the postwar period remade the lifestyle of American Jews, so that in many aspects Jews became part of the American establishment. This was particularly true in the realms of academic and artistic endeavor, where Jews became a dominant force during this era. It was thus no longer necessary to play down one's Jewishness or to make the defensive choice of highlighting it because the open society, within which older traditions, including the dominant Christian one, were clearly under attrition, was then making no assimilatory demands in the name of an American ideology."

The citation from the *Encyclopedia Judaica* printed above was published in 1972. Now, in the 1990s, a major upheaval has overtaken the Jewish community: Intermarriage, followed by assimilation, followed by disappearance of Jews *qua* Jews is proceeding at a rapid, dangerous rate. There are, of course, both Jews and Christians who do not care that this is so. They genuinely believe that a painless assimilation into the mainstream culture is a good thing, i.e., good for the Jews (no more discrimination, bigotry etc.) and good for the Christians (Jews are generally regarded as wise and successful, and their integration into the greater American society will strengthen America).

Of course, most Jews do not agree. They wish to see the continuity of the Jewish people; they wish to see their own children marry Jews and give them Jewish grandchildren; they wish for Jews to continue to make substantive contributions to society and civilization, and for the Jewish people to be recognized as the source from which these contributions stem.

They also do not wish to see the Nazis—and their admirers today—win a posthumous victory. The destruction of one-third of the Jewish people, it is felt, was a one-time catastrophe. The loss of more large numbers of Jews through intermarriage and assimilation would be a heavy, tragic blow.

Perhaps this older generation that is steadfast against assimilation and the disappearance of the Jewish people remembers an incident that took place in the early years of World War II. A Jewish delegation from the United States had succeeded in reaching India, and had requested and obtained an audience with Mahatma Ghandi, whose campaign for the liberation of India from the British Empire was moving toward a climactic, successful conclusion.

The Jewish delegation introduced themselves to the revered Indian leader and noted that by and large Jews throughout the world had supported his movement enthusiastically. Ghandi, it was reported, nodded in assent. The Jewish representatives now asked if he was aware of the horrible crimes the Germans

were committing against the Jews, who were being concen-
trated in death camps and labor camps. Again he nodded; he
knew.

The Jewish delegates then explained the reason for their
visit: Would Ghandi issue a statement, publicly and strongly
calling on the German government to cease and desist, and instead allow the imprisoned Jews to go free, and permit them
to emigrate?

There was a moment of silence, and a pause, and then
Ghandi replied.

I believe, he said, there is a much better way. I believe the
Jews in these wretched camps should commit mass suicide—
that will immediately alert the world to their plight.

As one man, the Jews rose and left. There was nothing more
to say.

What Ghandi apparently did not know was that the guid-
ing light and slogan of Judaism and the Jewish people is life,
not death.

The major source of Jewish immigration to the United
States dates to the late 1800s and the early 1900s. An estimated three million Jews were admitted to America in those
years. Most historians agree that the majority of these immigrants, primarily from eastern Europe, were poor people. The
rich and successful Jews remained behind. These poor immigrants, by and large, were observant Jews, but probably more
from habit than from knowledge. When they found that circumstances compelled them to work on the holy Sabbath day
of rest, they worked; their chief goal was to put food on the
family's table, and in general to improve their lot in the new
land.

When children came along, the sons were given a modicum
of religious education from the least-expensive school or tutor
they could find; in those days, girls did not receive any Jewish
religious education at all. At very tender ages, both boys and
girls were sent to work, and whatever they earned went into
the family's budget. It was rare that a son or daughter would
keep his earnings for himself.

The Jewish children who came to the United States as immigrants had to overcome their foreign accents, learn some basic arithmetic and American history, and then apply for citizenship. When the naturalization papers arrived from Washington, it was a day for celebration.

For those children born in America, there were other problems. Often the clothes they wore were hand-me-downs. If a parent were summoned to school—if there were a problem or to receive a commendation for a child—there was often embarrassment: for a parent's accent, or clothes, or obvious lack of education.

The east European Jews who arrived in America in the early 1900s loved their new homeland with a passion. There was free schooling, policemen who patrolled the streets and who were not pogrom-makers; if you worked hard you could save in a bank and gradually move to a better apartment, or buy better clothes, or send for another relative from the old country. Best of all, when you became a citizen, you could vote, just like everybody else. For most Jews from the small, fear-ridden towns, life in America—despite the poverty, the crowding, the noise, the gradual disappearance of some of the old religious traditions—was nevertheless a dream come true. It was a free country! Your son could study in a high school, and if he was a gifted boy he could even get a scholarship to go on to college. And your daughter, after high school, could work in a nice office, and not in the sweaty shop sewing skirts and blouses.

There was very little occasion for young immigrant Jews in those days to meet Christians. They lived with Jews, they went to school with Jews, all of their friends and neighbors and relatives were Jewish; the chances of intermarriage were close to zero.

And even when economic conditions improved for a Jewish family, which generally happened after they had lived in America for a few years, they tended to move to a better apartment in a virtually all-Jewish neighborhood. It was simply an old habit that was hard for them to get out of—they felt more comfortable, more secure, more relaxed living among fellow

Jews. They could chat in Yiddish, there were kosher food stores that catered to their needs, and they were sure that it was a good place for their children to meet and socialize with other Jewish youngsters, so that the danger of falling in love with a Christian was minimal.

By and large the generation of Jews born in America to immigrant parents turned out to be a very ambitious group. Unlike their parents, they fully understood the potential future that lay before them if they could get into a college and do well. Almost entirely on their own, they strove for high grades, and many of them excelled in their studies. They became lawyers, teachers, physicians, accountants. At least one of these immigrant children, Isidor Rabi, became a Nobel Prizewinner in Physics, and a science adviser to President Eisenhower. Others became writers (Alfred Kazin), performers (Danny Kaye). musicians; some even became rabbis, but mostly the American version—modern Orthodox, Conservative or Reform.

Often there was conflict between the newer generation and the older. One of the sons of the immigrant generation was born Wallechinsky; he turned to writing, and became the enormously successful fiction writer, Irving Wallace. When his son, Adam, was born, he, of course, received the best of everything.

And when Adam was old enough, he changed his name back to Wallechinsky—so that his identity would be clear and sharp and unambiguous.

Chapter XIII

Converts to Judaism Have a Message for Intermarrieds

PEOPLE—ESPECIALLY JEWS WHO ARE NOT CLOSE TO THEIR tradition—often wonder why some famous individuals, movie stars like Elizabeth Taylor, the late Marilyn Monroe, and the late Sammy Davis, Jr., choose to become Jewish. A case could be made for them remaining members of whichever Christian denomination they were born into, without the additional hassle and burden of turning Jewish.

Elizabeth Taylor, the story goes, converted to please her late husband, the producer Mike Todd, a rabbi's son. Marilyn Monroe, it is said, became Jewish because her husband at the time, the playwright Arthur Miller, suggested it. Sammy Davis, however, is an entirely different story. He explains in his own words why he converted:

> I'm a Jew and proud of it. I'd like very much to get the record straight—I became a Jew because it gave me an inner strength and was the answer to a curiosity that stalked me for many years.
>
> I started out in the backstage of a Broadway theater in the lower drawer of a dresser. My first birthday was celebrated in a specially contrived crib made up of suitcases in a dressing room at the old Hippodrome Theater in New York City.
>
> My mother, the former Elvita Sanchez, is a Catholic and my dad is a Baptist. Both gave me religious encouragement, although you wouldn't call us a churchgoing family.
>
> God must have put His arms around me that terrible day in 1954 when I was in a severe accident while driving from Las Vegas to Hollywood. Maybe it was in the hospital after the accident when it happened. Or maybe it was beginning to work before then, but the frustration of looking for that something meaningful in life began to work on me.
>
> As I lay on the stark white hospital bed, friends came and tried to give me encouragement. I remember the Jewish chaplain in the hospital stopping at my bed one morning and asking how I felt. I guess I started talking to him about what it was I was looking for in life. I was confused and admitted it. I was looking for something morally tangible. I had everything a fellow could want—all the material things in life, that is.
>
> Lying in that hospital bed, I began thinking out loud. I must have asked him a million questions about the miracle of my coming out of the accident alive. He listened intently, didn't give answers, but gave me a philosophy where I might find those answers. The chaplain was strong and gave me part of that strength.
>
> As soon as I was well enough to move around, I began asking the nurses about this chaplain. I told them how easy he was to understand. The head nurse smiled and commented, "Maybe that's why you'll never find a rabbi suffering from ulcers." We joked about it, but as I came to understand more and more about Judaism, that kidding remark made me think.

I was at the Fairmont Hotel in San Francisco a few years later, at a children's charity party. I love to entertain kids. After my act, I was seated at a table with a young man in his early thirties. I thought he was an entertainer and started to kid about my working benefits. He smiled warmly and commented, "I do this almost every day of the year."

"Gee," I said, "are things that bad?"

He chuckled good-naturedly and introduced himself. He was Rabbi Alvin I. Fine of Congregation Emanu-El. He pointed out that he had spent the best part of his life working with various organizations throughout California raising funds for needy groups.

He was like the rabbi I had met in the hospital. Everything he said had meaning, not just idle conversation. He spoke so convincingly that I told him he should be on the stage. He joked that he was, in a sense, and performed 365 days a year. "Could any actor match that?" he quipped.

Our casual conversation began to develop into a deep soul-searching experience. Once more my curiosity about Judaism was set aflame. I told him about the rabbi I had met in the hospital and how I was interested in learning more about Judaism. "But," I added, "I honestly haven't the time to sit down and read half a dozen books."

He adjusted the dark-framed glasses he wore with dignity and said, "Years ago another man had a similar problem. He asked the great Rabbi Hillel how he could learn as much as possible about Judaism as quickly as possible. Standing on one foot for a split second the man heard Hillel recite eleven words which gave him the complete philosophy of Judaism. Those eleven words were what we know today as the Golden Rule: *Do unto others as you would have others do unto you.*

With those words he smiled warmly, shook my hand, adding, "And here are the names of a few books that you may read that will explain those words." He told me I could reach him at his office anytime I was in San Francisco.

It was all too simple, I thought. And, despite the fact that I barely have enough time to sleep, I made it my business to get some of the books he put on that list. After checking with most of the libraries around Hollywood, all I could pick up were two volumes. I wrote to a friend in New York and told him what I was doing. He sent me two more books from his personal collection.

At first, reading those books confused me. I would read a few pages, close the book, and try to figure out what the writer was saying. Little by little I began to understand. That uncertain feeling that gnawed at my bones began to relax. Something was coming through and I wasn't confused anymore.

On my next trip to San Francisco I got in touch with Rabbi Fine again. I told him I had read every single one of the books he had suggested and had studied them until I was blue in the face. He chuckled and said, "Now you know more than half of my congregation does. Come over and deliver the sermon this *Shabbes.*" I almost called his bluff but couldn't make it that Saturday. I did go to his temple a few days later. It was the first time I had been in a Reform temple.

I walked toward the rostrum and saw the simple wood cabinet covered with dark red velvet; embroidered on the velvet was a replica of the tablets Moses carried down from Mount Sinai.

My friend pressed a light switch, pulled the curtain gently, and revealed the contents. Inside I saw four satin-covered scrolls, with silver crown-like ornaments on top of each, resting against a board covered with plain blue velvet. It was one of the most majestic sights I have ever seen.

Rabbi Fine told me that within those scrolls lay the writings of the sages of old, the history of the Jewish people, and the laws and customs by which they live. He explained how only a small section of the scroll is read each week at services so that everyone can relive history and gain a greater appreciation of life today. Rabbi Fine said, "It is a guidepost, a ruler, a staff from which we learn. Men have spent a lifetime studying the Torah, and when they drew their last breath they confessed their only regret was that they could not finish their work."

A year passed. Some close Jewish friends thought I was crazy for even thinking about becoming a Jew; others approved of my plans. I realized I wanted to become a Jew because it gave me a great strength, and because I felt it gave me the answer to an inner peace in life. For me, Judaism held an honesty and spiritual peace that were lacking in my personal makeup. I wanted to become Jewish because the customs of Judaism hold a cleanliness that no other philosophy on this earth can offer. Judaism for me meant security and understanding, and was an answer to my confusion and uncertainty. I wanted to become a Jew because I wanted to share something with my fellow man, who has been sharing with me. And because I believe that God is on our side.

The greatest thrill of my life (was) the day I walked out of the temple as a Jew. I became a Jew because I was ready and willing to understand the plight of a people who fought for thousands of years for a homeland, giving their lives and bodies, and finally gaining that homeland.

Now, several years later, how does it feel to be a Jew? I can only answer briefly, like Rabbi Hillel—"It's me, that's all, just me and the way I see life and enjoy living." Shalom!

Why would a Roman Catholic priest from England convert to Judaism, and become not only an Orthodox, observant Jew, but a teacher of Talmud in a Jewish day school?

Let Abraham Carmel tell it in his own way:

I began, after seven years in the priesthood, to doubt seriously and painfully the cornerstone dogma of orthodox Christianity, in particular, the divinity of Jesus. Had there been no other problems I should simply have become a single-minded Unitarian. . . . I came across the works of Professor Joseph Klausner. This very erudite and masterful writer, in his book *From Jesus to Paul,* related in a compelling manner the early origins of Christianity and demonstrated how the teachings of a simple Jewish "rabbi" had evolved or developed into a dogmatic system within the framework of a vast Caesar-like organization.

As a result of this and many other writings of a similar nature, as well as a complete review of history, I regretfully came to the firm conclusion that the real founder of Christianity as we know it was not Jesus but Saul of Tarsus, who was later to become the great missionary Paul. This genius desired to take religion to the Gentile world. He was the greatest missionary in history. Moreover, in his brilliance he realized that the Gentile world could not embrace monotheistic Judaism. So he blended it with Hellenistic forms and ideas, rendering it palatable to a world unaccustomed to pure religion. This led me to examine the source from which Christianity and, later Islam, sprang, namely, Judaism, the mother faith.

Here I found not a creed or system of beliefs but a way of life. Here were no dogmas or mystery to swallow, but a simple yet profound revelation from God Himself to a people chosen by

Him to be the bearers, for all time, of His vital message. Every department of daily life, from morn till eve, was related to, identified with, and saturated by this way-of-life religion.

Finally I decided that I wished to become identified with this true revelation and God-given way of life. But this was the trouble—Judaism does not want proselytes. This is even more true in British Jewry than in American. The London Beth Din is the strictest in the world. It would require a special article to relate the difficulties encountered with this formidable body. In a word, it took five years to batter my way through the doors of the Anglo-Jewish Ecclesiastical Court of Rabbis.

Meanwhile, my conscience would not permit me to continue in the priesthood. So I walked out. I had no security, no promises, no job, no income. All I had was faith in God. I found a job in a private Episcopalian boarding school. Here I ate only vegetables and tried to keep Shabbat. Eventually, the Beth Din accepted me and I went to teach at the great Anglo-Jewish school, Carmel College, near Oxford. Here I taught English and Latin and prepared for my reception into Judaism. My eight years at Carmel College were inspiring and rewarding.

At the end of eight years I felt an urge to work in Israel, the land that the God of our fathers had miraculously restored to us. So once again I packed my bags and set off on this new stage of my spiritual journey. I taught at the Reali high school in Haifa and found the very lively sabras true friends and excellent pupils. I loved Israel, but my health failed. Acting upon medical advice, I returned to England, where I regained my health.

I was invited to visit America and lost no time in fulfilling an ambition of many years. I fell in love with America and recognized in this fortress of democracy a most desirable land. In the course of my lecturing I became acquainted with many great institutions, both Jewish and non-Jewish. I should like to give some idea of the questions put to me, as well as my answers.

My main concern with American-Jewish life is the youth. Here is the weakest link in the communal chain. With energy and vision it could become its strongest pillar. Above all, the student body needs urgent attention. On the campuses I found hundreds of students in a complete spiritual fog. They simply have no idea of Judaism or even of Jewishness. Our grand traditions have no meaning for them, and they are marching quickly from apathy to apostasy.

Intermarriage will mean the loss of their children to any form of Jewishness. The B'nai B'rith Hillel Foundations are doing magnificent work, but they need powerful allies if they are to become effective in more than the social sphere. I respectfully suggest that for the next decade a very substantial portion of the material and moral reserves of the American-Jewish community should be invested in its youth. No project is as vital; none will pay richer dividends.

Of the hundreds of questions posed to me during my tour, three or four constantly recurred. They follow:

• *What is your attitude now towards the Catholic Church?*

Answer: One of great respect and admiration. I have never uttered a word of attack against the church.

• *How can we convert Jews to Judaism?*

Answer: First, restore a sense of pride to unaffiliated or assimilated Jews in Jewishness. The State of Israel is a powerful instrument in this regard. Jews are no longer spiritual or moral outcasts. By God's mercy, we again have our universal center. Second, Jewish schools need full support so that a new generation will know, cherish and practice the great way of life handed down by our fathers.

• *Should we try to convert non-Jews?*

Answer: I oppose Jewish missionary activities. We Jews believe that all righteous men, of whatever faith, will be saved. Accepting Judaism is a serious responsibility, and is not to be dealt with lightly. Let us concentrate on "should-be" Jews before dealing with "would-be" Jews.

A recent work of world Jewish history, written by a Christian scholar and historian, who obviously possesses a great admiration for the Jewish people, has made an impact on young Jewish readers, especially those who know little if anything of their people's history. In his book, simply titled *A History of the Jews,* Paul Johnson stresses that not only did the ancient Jews "invent ethical monotheism" but they also introduced to humanity the concepts of equality under the law, and democratic philosophy.

He goes further and insists that the Jewish people played—

and still play—a major role in the creation of the modern world, from the introduction of secular ideas, the evolution of capitalism, the exploration of the psyche and the revolutionary development of twentieth-century culture.

Johnson demonstrates the interconnection between Jewish history and western history, and between the philosophical, ethical, religious, social and political notions of Jewish culture and its impact on the western world.

One of the reasons that he decided to write a history of the Jews, Johnson explains, is because the Jewish people—almost from its earliest beginnings—believed that man's sojourn on earth has a reason and a purpose, and a destiny. This is still a powerful Jewish sentiment. As Johnson puts it: "At a very early stage in (the Jews') collective existence they believed they had detected a divine scheme for the human race, of which their own society was to be a pilot. They worked out their role in immense detail. They clung to it with heroic persistence in the face of savage suffering. Many (Jews) believe it still . . . The Jews stand at the center of the perennial attempt to give human life the dignity of a purpose."

It is estimated that about half of all the Jews in the United States are unaffiliated with any Jewish institution. They are not members of a synagogue, they do not contribute to the local Jewish community fund that provides support for local needs, Jews in distress overseas, and for aid to Israel in absorbing and resettling immigrants from various parts of the world. These Jews do not belong to B'nai B'rith, Hadassah, or any of the smaller Jewish organizations. In other words, their link to Judaism and/or the Jewish people is virtually nil.

What these people have not done is formally convert to Christianity or any other faith. Of course, it is from this sector that intermarriage garners its greatest numbers. And although there are no precise figures, most specialists studying the phenomenon of the cults and the Christian missionary groups in the United States believe that the majority of the young Jewish men and women who wind up in cult groups, or join so-called Hebrew-Christian congregations, or affiliate with Jews for Jesus, come from this reservoir of unaffiliated, unconnected and—generally—Jewishly ignorant group.

What keeps these people Jewish? For one thing, anti-Semitism. They are generally very sensitive to subtle forms of anti-Semitism, and react to it sharply. Another is often nostalgia: they remember affectionately early years when a deceased parent provided them with a loving ambience, and certain Jewish foods still hold a special place in their memory book. These people usually believe that Judaism and Jewish life, and even modern Israel, are old-fashioned, a vestige of old country memories. They fail to understand that being Jewish entails constant study, and that Judaism strongly believes in the reality of life on earth as we know it—and that each person has an obligation to contribute to society, for the benefit of all people. If one were to dig deep, chances are that the overwhelming majority of Jews in this unaffiliated category either had no Jewish educational training whatsoever, or if they did it was so inferior that it actually turned people away from all contact with Judaism.

Happily, in recent years there has been a growing group of educated, intelligent young men and women who sensed that being ignorant of Judaism, and remaining unaffiliated with the Jewish people, they were missing out on a vital dimension of their lives, and they have begun to study intensively, to make up for what they saw as lost years.

The late Paul Cowan, whose father was a major executive with the Columbia Broadcasting System, and whose mother came from an assimilated, very wealthy family, was brought up totally devoid of Judaism. He married a Gentile girl; and then—being highly intelligent—they both realized that there was something essential missing. Rachel converted to Judaism, Paul and his wife became observant, and the two of them inspired countless numbers of intermarried, unaffiliated young Jews to follow them on the road back to Jewish life.

Tragically, Paul died at a very early age; his widow has become a Reform rabbi. The work of bringing young American Jews back to Judaism continues.

As one rabbi quipped, perhaps only half in jest, fifty years ago Jews were discriminated against, and there was no intermarriage. Today, they are accepted, according to the latest surveys, and intermarriage is on the upswing. (Fifty years ago a Jewish young woman looking for a sales job in a department store would sometimes wear a crucifix to help her get the job. Today, any sign of discrimination would be reported immediately, and might even be the basis for a suit against the offender).

In the new book *Saving Remnants: Feeling Jewish in America,* by Sara Bershtel and Allen Graubard, the authors sought to find out about the inner life of the estimated two and a half-million unaffiliated American Jews. Why are they so unconnected to Judaism and Jewish life? Or, to put it another way— is their disaffiliation with Judaism just another way of being a very modern, sophisticated American? After all, in America, no one is coerced into going to church or synagogue; and more and more interreligious and interracial marriages seem to be taking place all around us. So, is this disaffiliation simply a sign of the future? Is the unconnected Jew a harbinger of things to come in America, in the 1990s and beyond?

The authors of this highly readable volume are well aware of the two schools of thought that prevail in America today vis-a-vis the American Jewish community: one school says that because of intermarriage and assimilation, the size of the community will shrink rapidly in the next few generations; the opposing viewpoint is that there is a hard core of committed, observant American Jews who will continue the Jewish tradition in America, and although the quantity of American Jews in future years may be smaller than it is at present, the quality will be far superior.

But Bershtel and Graubard have found an entirely different subculture of unaffiliated Jews. Some of these disaffiliated Jews are fearful of a new Holocaust, this time in America, and are making plans (shrinking their funds to portable diamonds, or learning how to handle pistols and rifles). Some of these unaffiliated Jews sprang from ultra-leftist circles, and were at first highly critical of Israel for what they perceived to be anti-Arab practices, until they realized that the anti-Israel stance of some of their colleagues was a form of old-fashioned anti-Semitism. They were also shocked and troubled deeply by thinly disguised anti-Semitism that developed in the Black community. These still left-leaning Jews, who have no interest in Judaism or Israel, nevertheless are no longer quite as unaffiliated as they used to be, as a result of unabashed anti-Semitism, and a deep fear of another Holocaust.

Bershtel and Graubard also note that among these still alienated Jews, certain other odd changes have been taking place. Years ago, these unconnected Jews would have sneered at a traditional bar or bat mitzvah, but today some of these people are conducting what they call a secular bar or bat mitzvah, or even a "radical" bar or bat mitzvah. A wedding takes place involving a Jewish groom and a Christian bride (it's a second wedding for both). There is a rabbi and a minister in attendance, and surprisingly a klezmer band, invoking—for the Jews present at least—memories of old European hamlets, with their klezmer orchestras and traditional Jewish music.

In the 1990s, it seems, there are gay-lesbian synagogues; there are intermarried couples who try to persuade both sets of parents that their bonding, between a Jew and a Christian, is really a step closer to a happier, more peaceful world where universal brotherhood will reign. There are even worshipers in traditional, Orthodox synagogues who confess that they do not believe in God, but they enjoy the services, the sermon, the feeling of camaraderie, the fellowship. (Some voice the hope that perhaps one day soon they will be able to say they do believe in God).

As the twenty-first century hovers over the horizon, it seems clearer every day that the Jewish community in America—if it is to preserve its uniqueness, and continue to afford its members a deeply satisfying religious and spiritual life—must tackle the issue of intermarriage and assimilation with courage, imagination and determination. The problem will not go away by itself.

Chapter XIV

Judaism Is a Tree of Life—Hold on to It!

ONE HUNDRED YEARS AGO, IN EASTERN EUROPE, WHEN LIFE sometimes seemed just too difficult, what with pogroms, abject poverty, little hope on the horizon, depressing news of Jewish communities overseas, one Jew would look at another, sigh deeply, and mutter, *Oy vay*. And the other, often with a twinkle in the eye, would respond, *Siz shver tsu zein a yid* (It's tough to be a Jew).

And yet, despite all obstacles, all problems, Jews to an overwhelmingly large degree remained Jews, at least in the small towns and hamlets in eastern Europe, which included Russia, Poland, the Baltic states, Romania, Hungary, and Czechoslovakia. Those Jews living in western societies like Germany, France, Britain and the United States, especially those who had been residents of those areas for several generations, were known to be gradually intermarrying, assimilating and disappearing. This was not true of the religiously committed Jews, or of the fervently Zionist Jews, but of those who felt that for them Judaism was merely an appendage, something that could be dropped without too much harm following in its wake.

The situation of the American Jewish community in the 1990s is very complex, and requires careful consideration.

For example:
- There are cult groups and Christian missionaries actively seeking to persuade young Jews, and sometimes elderly Jews too, to abandon Judaism and affiliate with them. In the two decades from the early 1970s to the 1990s an estimated one hundred thousand American Jews have been ensnared by cults and missions. Thousands of Jewish families have been affected; some of these families accept the tragic situation, while others regard themselves as utterly destroyed.
- Cults and missionaries generally target those Jews who know little or nothing about Judaism. In recent years one of their favorite targets has been the Russian Jews who arrived in America almost totally devoid of any knowledge of Judaism, Jewish history, Jewish culture.
- Simultaneous with this confrontational problem has been awareness within the Jewish community that anti-Semitism in the United States has been growing. After news of the Holocaust encompassed all Jews at the end of World War II, there was a kind of unspoken, unwritten gentleman's agreement—the world felt it was unseemly for anti-Semitism to go public so soon after news of the Nazi massacre of six million Jews. But now, a half-century later, this ugly cancer on mankind's soul has erupted again—not only from the neo-Nazis, extreme rightists and anyone else who is sick with bigotry, but also, to most Jews' shock, from the Black community, especially the educated, politically aware circles

within the Black community. To say that American Jews are shocked, confused, fearful and worried by these developments is an understatement.

- Although Israel is believed by most Jews to be strong and capable of withstanding any enemy assaults, most American Jews remain deeply worried about her welfare and well-being. There is a great dichotomy here: Jews living in the free countries are thrilled to learn that hundreds of thousands of Russian Jews, most of them highly educated, have reached safe haven in Israel, together with thousands of impoverished Ethiopian Jews, all of whom will continue to need substantial aid so that they all can be absorbed into the social and economic life of the Jewish state. Despite the great pride taken in these achievements, and the confidence that given a little time, Israel will become a beacon of light—not only benefiting all mankind with scientific and medical advances, but also acting as a catalyst to all Jews around the world—as they seek to strengthen their spiritual life . . . despite all this, concern for Israel's safety and security remains high on Jews' agenda.

- And in the face of everything else, the single most worrisome item on the Jewish community's agenda is intermarriage, assimilation and disappearance. The numbers of intermarried, i.e., Jews who marry non-Jews who do not convert to Judaism, and who do not raise their children as Jews, are staggering.

For those parents who do not really care about this development, and happily accept a Gentile son-in-law or daughter-in-law, and their families and future grandchildren, this book has no message. These parents are themselves already at least half-assimilated, and well on their way to leaving the Jewish community. We are sad to see them go, especially after the unprecedented losses of the Holocaust. We wish them all well.

Possibly some day, somehow, one of the intermarried Gentiles will decide to convert to Judaism, and will bring the Jewish spouse along, and re-establish a truly Jewish family. Perhaps it will work the other way, and the Jewish partner in the marriage will decide that after all is said and done, he/she wants a Jewish family, and will urge the non-Jewish partner to convert.

Who knows what may happen? A visit to Israel may trigger a warm response. A book, a play, a lecture, a meeting with an impressive Jew—anything and everything may change people's minds in the future. When David Ben-Gurion was prime minister of Israel, his only son lay wounded in a hospital, and was nursed back to health by a British Christian young woman. Love followed, and Amos, the son, notified his father they were marrying. The prime minister sent along a note and a Bible, wishing them well; several months later, the young lady converted; today no one even remembers that she was once not Jewish.

But what of those parents who do care that their children intermarry? And what of the young people themselves? How to reach them, and try very hard to persuade them to transform the new-family-to-be into a Jewish family?

How does one explain to a young person in love that when they marry, it is not only the young woman or young man they are binding their lives to but their families, and their histories, and their cultures?

How does one stress the words that will show that while Christianity is a religion, Judaism is a whole way of life— and are the Jews caught up in this dilemma ready to surrender a soul-filling, deeply-satisfying way of life in exchange for a religion whose practitioners undoubtedly find being a Christian easier than being a Jew.

How little Jews know about Judaism! After all, the knowledge, the lore, the wisdom, all of it has been accruing for some 4,000 years.

One can spend a lifetime studying the Hebrew Bible and the Talmud, and comparing the commentaries that have accumulated through the centuries, and come to realize that one lifetime is really not enough to absorb all this material.

I glance around at my home library, and wonder how many young Jews have read some of these books, and if they have left any kind of impact on them. Books like *Jewish Contributions to*

Civilization by Cecil Roth, *What Does Judaism Say About. . .?* by Louis Jacobs, *The Diary of a Young Girl* by Anne Frank, the autobiographical works of Elie Wiesel, Yitzhak Rabin, Abba Eban, the biographies of Chaim Weizmann, David Ben-Gurion, Louis D. Brandeis, *While Six Million Jews Died* by Arthur Morse, *The Abandonment of the Jews* by David Wyman, *The War Against the Jews,* by Lucy Davidowicz, *My People,* by Abba Eban, *The Source* by James Michener.

Some of the most inspiring, beautiful passages in the English language appear in the Hebrew Bible (both the 1917 masoretic translation and the new 1985 translation), in the daily and Sabbath prayerbook, in the special High Holy Days prayerbook. When was the last time you glanced, or read, or were touched?

It took a non-Jewish professor to coin a phrase that Jews appreciate (It is the title of his book *The Jewish Mystique* by Ernst van den Haag.): Is there a *Jewish mystique* about the Jewish people? Probably. By now, whatever this is, it has become part of our culture and national personality.

To be a Jew means to enjoy life (there are some religions that do not stress this), to be ethical to the nth degree (probably all faiths emphasize this point), to learn and teach and set an example, to be kind and compassionate, peaceful and hospitable, and continue during all of one's life to make this world a better place than when you first entered it. Are these last points especially Jewish traits? Perhaps. Perhaps not. But if *you* were born into this ancient, remarkable people; if *you* do not wish to sever the link that connects *you* to your parents and grandparents—all the way back to Moses, the Patriarchs and Matriarchs—then it behooves you to consider very carefully before taking the serious, fateful step of giving up Judaism and the Jewish people.

Being Jewish can be a source of enormous joy and satisfaction. But like anything, this goal—of being a committed, knowledgeable, understanding Jew—takes work and effort. That includes a weekly Sabbath pause, a time for meditation, prayer, song and family togetherness; and recognition of the festivals and holidays (Tu B'shvat, Arbor Day; Purim, marking Queen Esther's saving of the Jewish people; Passover, commemorating the exodus from Egypt, the oldest holiday in Western civilization; Shavuot, marking the giving of the Torah to Moses on Sinai; the solemn High Holy Days of Rosh Hashanah and Yom Kippur; and the Sukkot festival, when the last harvest of the season took place in ancient days; Hanukkah, the joyous festival, when the Temple was rededicated, and Judaism was saved). Nowadays we have additional holidays: Israel Independence Day, Jerusalem Reunification Day, and the mournful fast day of Tisha B'av, when we recall the destruction of both the first and second Holy Temples.

Mind you, celebrating the Sabbath and the holidays is only a part of Jewish life. Time must be allocated for study, for organized charity for the needy, for worship services and the sense of fellowship that ensues. If one is blessed, a family will celebrate a child's birth (with a circumcision ceremony for a boy) and a special celebration for a girl; there will also be religious school classes, a bar/bat mitzvah, an engagement party, a wedding. In times of tragedy, Judaism provides for a time for mourning, and Jewish mourners have found that the mourning laws and customs that have evolved over the centuries do comfort the mourner.

The aforementioned are mere headings of what Jewish life comprises. It cannot easily be summarized on the printed page, or on the television screen. One should live Jewish life, slowly perhaps at first, and then let it evolve.

Every Sabbath morning at services the Torah is removed from the Holy Ark, unrolled, read aloud, rerolled, returned to the Ark, and the whole congregation sings together: "(The Torah) is a Tree of Life for those who hold fast to it." But one must first extend one's hands, read and study the Torah, make it a part of one's life.

For a Jewish person to—in effect—push the Torah away, and walk away from Judaism and the Jewish people, and from a beautiful, happiness-producing way of life would be not only tragic but also foolish.

Judaism is a spiritual treasure, waiting only to be shared and enjoyed, and passed on.

SOME USEFUL ADDRESSES

1. If a member of your family, or someone you know well, is involved with a cult, two groups that will help are:

International Cult Educational Program
P.O. Box 1232 Gracie Station
New York, N.Y. 10028 (Tel. 212–439-1550)

Task Force on Missionaries and Cults
Att: Dr. Philip Abramowitz
Jewish Community Relations Council of New York
12th Floor, 711 Third Avenue
New York, N.Y. 10017 (Tel. 212–983-4800)

2. To contact a Jewish group:

You may join a synagogue (Orthodox, Conservative, Reform or Reconstructionist). For newly-married couples, many synagogues offer low, initial membership rates.

You may also join a Jewish Community Center, a
YMHA-YWHA, a local branch of B'nai B'rith, Hadassah, Amit, Emunah, Na'amat, B'nai Zion. There are also
professional Jewish clubs, e.g., for Jewish policemen in
New York City (Shomrim Society), for Jewish firemen
(Ner Tamid Society), as well as groups for physicians, at-
torneys and accountants. Here it is best to inquire from a
colleague in the same field.

In large urban areas, Boy Scouts have a Jewish-oriented
troop; in New York there is even a "Jewish Motorcycle
Club."

The rabbi of your local synagogue, or the executive direc-
tor of the local Y or Community Center, will be happy to
help with an address or phone.

RECOMMENDED READING

Herman Wouk, *This Is My God* (Walker). The acclaimed novelist explains his understanding of Judaism and Jewish observances.

W. Gunther Plaut, *The Torah: A Modern Commentary.* (Union of American Hebrew Congs.) A leading Reform rabbi cites numerous Jewish and general sources and makes understanding the first section of the Hebrew Bible clear and enjoyable.

David C. Gross, *How To Be Jewish* (Hippocrene) Straightforwardly, the reader is led through a series of steps that lead to understanding of what being Jewish really means.

Irving Greenberg, *The Jewish Way: Living the Holidays* (Summit). Jewish life is explained through celebration of the Jewish festivals.

David Wyman, *The Abandonment of the Jews* (Pantheon). A non-Jewish historian recounts in chilling detail how the United States turned its back on European Jewry during the Nazi era.

Francine Klagsbrun, *Voices of Wisdom* (Godine). A stimulating collection of Jewish textual excerpts to guide the reader toward ideals and ethics for everyday living.

Cecil Roth, *Jewish Contributions to Civilization* (East/West Library). Vignettes of outstanding Jews in a wide range of fields who have had a great impact on world civilization.

Holy Scriptures (masoretic translation), *Tanakh* (1985 new translation, Jewish Publication Society). The full Hebrew Bible, in English or in Hebrew and English.

Paul Johnson, *A History of the Jews* (Harper & Row). A scholar's remarkable retelling of nearly four millenia of Jewish history, filled with insights and memorable details.

David C. Gross, *Judaism* (Hippocrene). A description of what the Jewish religion represents, stressing its dedication to deeds and ideals.

Louis Jacobs, *What Does Judaism Say About. . .?* (Quadrangle). A noted British rabbi's responses to questions about marriage, abortion, ESP, homosexuality, psychoanalysis, ecumenism, ecology, astrology, and more.

Paul Cowan, *An Orphan in History* (Anchor Books). A triumphant ending of one American Jew who searched for and discovered his roots.

Lucy Davidowicz, *The War Against the Jews 1933–1945* (Holt, Rinehart & Winston). The noted historian records the unimaginable, calculated Nazi campaign to destroy the world's Jewish population.

Neil Gillman, *Sacred Fragments* (Jewish Publication Society). This noted philosophy professor at the Jewish Theological Seminary tackles tough questions: How do we know God exists? Why do we need ritual?

Joseph Telushkin, *Jewish Literacy* (Morrow). A collection of short pieces described as "the most important things to know about the Jewish religion, its people and its history."

Nathan Ausubel. *A Treasury of Jewish Folklore* (Crown). A memorable assembly of old country stories, traditions, legends, humor, wisdom and folk songs of the Jewish people.

Ethics of the Talmud (Pirke Aboth). Edited and translated by B.

Travers Herford (Schocken). A never-ending source of guidance on ethical behavior.

Connor Cruise O'Brein, *The Siege* (Simon & Schuster). A powerful history of Israel, told by a distinguished scholar and editor.

David C. Gross, *1201 Questions and Answers About Judaism* (Hippocrene). Frequently-asked questions about every conceivable aspect of Judaism, with brief, factual replies.

David C. Gross, *The Jewish People's Almanac* (Hippocrene). A potpourri of short articles encompassing Jewish life in America, around the world, with biographies, unusual holiday celebrations, past and present.

INDEX

Abraham, 82
AIDS, 89
Alexandria, 58
American Jewish Committee, 95
American Legion, 45
American Nazism, 93
American Technion Society, 126
Anti-Semitism, 19
Atheism, 50
Aufruf, 87

Ba'alei T'shuvah, 12
Baptism, 3
Bayme, Steven, 95
Ben-Gurion, David, 14
Berger, Rabbi Philmore, 91
Bershtel, Sara, 154
Blood libel, 26
Brandeis, Louis D., 46, 117
Brandeis University, 96
Branover, Prof. Herman, 124
Buber, Martin, 39
Buchwald, Rabbi Ephraim, 62

Cabal, 27
Cardin, Shoshanah, 129
Carmel, Abraham, 149
Cassandras, 112
Chanukah, 54
Chilean purchasing mission, 115
Christian dogma, 100
Christian minister, 76
Christian partners, 77
Christmas tree, 84
Circumcision, 55
Cleveland, 75
Cohen, Dr. Gerson, 130
Commentary, 102
Convent, 18

Conversion, 9
Coughlin, Father, 45
Council of Jewish Federations, 73
Cowan, Paul, 83
Cowan, Rachel, 48
Credos, 70
Czarist fake, 25

Daily Forward, 33
Davidowicz, Lucy, 49, 131
Davis, Sammy, Jr., 145
Discrimination, 15
Dreyfus, Alfred, 137

Einstein, Albert, 71
Eisenstein, Ira, 104
El Al, 36
Eliav, Aryeh, 50
Encyclopedia Judaica, 139
Epstein, Rabbi Jerome, 86
Ethical will, 64
Ethics of the Fathers, 67
Ezra, 42

Fein, Prof. Leonard, 130
Fleg, Edmond, 20
France, 4
Freud, Sigmund, 39

Gallup Poll, 63
Geneva, 22
Genocide, 80
Gentile, 80
Get (religious divorce), 9
Ghandi, Mahatma, 154
Goldwater, Sen. Barry, 81
Grant, Ulysses S., 45
Graubard, Allen, 154

Hadassah, 127
Haifa, 35
Halacha, 18
Harvard, 22
Hasidic way, 57
Hawaii, 62
Hebrew language, 4
Heine, Heinrich, 3
Herberg, Will, 99
Herzl, Theodor, 118
Herzog, Chaim, 21
Heschel, Rabbi Abraham Joshua, 128
Hillel Centers, 52
Hillel, Rabbi, 69
Hoffer, Erich, 90
Holocaust denial, 117
Holocaust Museum, 5
Holocaust survivors, 2
Holy Temple, 42

Iceland, 36
Identity, 29
Intermarriage rites, 47
"Irreligious," 99
Isaac, 82
Israeli rabbinate, 78

Jacob, 82
Jacobs, Dr. Louis, 41
Jerusalem Report, 95
Jewish Book Council, 138
Jewish prayerbook, 101
Jews for Jesus, 84
Johnson, Paul, 151
Joint Distribution Committee, 33
Joseph, 81
Josephus, 48

Kahane, Rabbi Meir, 12
Kaplan, Rabbi Mordecai M., 68

Kaye, Danny, 144
Kazin, Alfred, 144
Kennedy, President, 113
Kissinger, Henry, 113
Kol Nidre 28
Kosher restaurant, 26
Kushner, Rabbi Harold, 66

Lamm, Dr. Norman, 52, 102
Landsman, 28
Lauder, Ronald, 111
Lieberman, Sen. Joseph I., 14
Lincoln Center Synagogue, 62
Lipton, Robert, 130

Maimonides, 68
Matlins, Stuart, 116
Matza, 89
Mayer, Dr. Egon, 61
Messiah, 90
Meyer, Dr. Michael, 37
Middle Ages, 32
Miller, Arthur, 146
MIT, 125
Monroe, Marilyn, 145
Morgenthau, Henry, Jr., 111
Moses, 81
Moslem countries, 2
Moving to Israel, 57
Moyers, Bill, 41

Neighborhoods, 35
Nepal, 27
Newman, 30
Newsweek, 95
New York,, 109
Nobel Laureates, 58

Original sin, 100
Passover seder, 122
Plaut, Rabbi W. Gunther, 107

Index

Poland, 3
Prager, Dennis, 92
Proselytizing, 48

Rabbi (Nazi soldier's son), 10
Rabi, Isidor, 144
Rackman, Rabbi Emanuel, 105
Ransom, 32
Rebecca, 82
Reisman, Lawrence M., 58
Religion, 23
"Religious," 98
Roosevelt, President Franklin, 113
Rosenzweig, Franz, 3
Roth, Cecil, 9
Routtenberg, Rabbi Max, 106
Rubinger, Rabbi Ephraim, 92

Sabbath, 22
Salk, Jonas, 71
Sanhedrin, 44
Satan, 89
Scientology, 84
Sephardic Jews, 140
Shulchan Aruch, 68
Silverstein, Rabbi Alan, 85
Six Day War, 39
Soloveichik, Rabbi Joseph, 124
Spain, 79
Spirit of St. Louis, 46
Steinberg, Rabbi Milton, 98
Steinsaltz, Rabbi Adin, 59
Stuyvesant, Peter, 45
Survey of Jewish Community, 8
Swope, Gerard, 125
Switzerland, 18
Synagogue bylaws, 10

Tallit, 11
Taylor, Elizabeth, 145
Technion, 126
Television, 79
Telushkin, Rabbi Joseph, 92
Thirteen Principles, 68
Prof. Gary Tobin, 96
Mike Todd, 146
Toller, Ernst, 139
Torah, 71

United Jewish Appeal, 127
U.S. Army, 38
U.S. National Jewish Population Survey, 73
U.S. Supreme Court, 38
United Synagogue of Conservative Judaism, 86
Universal Brotherhood, 102

Vatican, 89
Venice, 32

Waldheim, Kurt, 111
Wallace, Irving, 144
Wallechinsky, 144
Wallenberg, Raoul, 112
White Lie, 6
Wiesel, Elie, 19
Wolfson, Prof. Harry, 84
Wouk, Herman, 133

Yad Vashem Memorial, 29
Yalow, Dr. Rosalyn
Yahrzeit, 54
Yarmulkes, 52
Yom Kippur, 27
Yogoslavia, 43

HIPPOCRENE GREAT RELIGIONS OF THE WORLD
James Haskins, General Editor

A series offering historical accounts of a wide array of religious groups active in the world today

THE MORMON CHURCH by *Roger Thompson*
The Mormons' struggle to establish a settlement in America and to define their beliefs is lucidly captured in this thorough account.
0-7818-0126-5   210 pages $14.95 hc

THE CATHOLIC CHURCH by *Barrie R. Straus*
"Exceptional...highly recommended."—*ALA Booklist*
0-7818-0070-6   288 pages $9.95 pb

THE BAPTISTS by *Anne Devereaux Jordan and R.M. Stifle*
"Inviting."—*ALA Booklist*
0-87052-784-3   160 pages $14.95

THE EPISCOPAL CHURCH by *David Locke*
"Particularly fascinating....Those who find contemporary controversies of interest will enjoy reading of the church's response to feminist and gay movements in America."—*ALA Booklist*
0-87052-900-5   256 pages $14.95

THE METHODISTS by *James Haskins*
"A good addition to the material currently available. Recommended."
—*Publishers Weekly*
0-7818-029-3   250 pages $14.95

RELIGIONS OF THE WORLD (2nd Edition) by *James Haskins*
The renowned writer and educator James Haskins considers the main tenets and practices of Christianity, Judaism, Hinduism, Buddhism, and Islam.
0-87052-930-7   252 pages $14.95

All prices subject to change.

Order directly from HIPPOCRENE BOOKS by sending a check or mail order for the price of the book, plus $4.00 shipping and handling for the first book, and $.50 for each additional book to:
HIPPOCRENE BOOKS, 171 MADISON AVE., NEW YORK, NY 10016

THE MOST COMPREHENSIVE ACCOUNT
OF JEWISH RELATIONS WITH POLAND
EVER PUBLISHED

JEWS IN POLAND
A Documentary History

Iwo Cyprian Pogonowski

Introduction by Professor Richard Pipes
of Harvard University

This eye-opening and monumental work describes the rise of Jews as a nation and how the Polish-Jewish community played a key role in this development. The book details the progress from the autonomous Congressus Judaicus to the Knesset in Israel. Pogonowski describes how the Congressus Judaicus was the only Jewish Parliament between the Sanhedrin of Biblical times and the Knesset of the modern State of Israel and thus, how the Jewish legal, governmental, and educational systems, as well as philosophical and religious beliefs, evolved in Poland between the 16th and 18th centuries.

Jews in Poland includes a new English translation of the Charter of Jewish Liberties and an illustrated description of the cultural, social, and political issues of the 500 years of Jewish autonomy in Poland. Pogonowski shows that during the entire history of the Diaspora, the Jewish nation existed only in Poland—with their own culture, social classes, and legal and economic systems—the Jews referred to the country as the "New Holy Land."

The book includes a detailed chronicle of the Holocaust, with ample annotations explaining the war-time situation.

384 pages 172 b/w photos 114 historical maps
0-7818-0116-8 $22.50 hc

JUDAICA HIGHLIGHTS FROM HIPPOCRENE

GOLEM *by G. Meyrink*
This version of the traditional Hebrew tale of a clay figure endowed with life was first published in 1915 and remains a classic today.
0-946626-12-X $11.95 pb

CHOOSING JUDAISM *by L. Kukoff*
This book is for those who have already come to Judaism through conversion as well as for those considering it. In his introduction, Rabbi Daniel Syme says of author Lydia Kukoff: "She makes a difference in the way people see themselves and their future as Jews...it is must reading for Jewish spouses, in-laws, rabbis, educators, congregational leaders—indeed for any thinking, caring Jew."
"Interesting and touching, splendid advice"—*Jewish News*
0-87052-070-9 $7.95 pb

THE CHRISTIAN PROBLEM:
A Jewish View *by Stuart E. Rosenberg*
This book is most timely as it raises questions that must be addressed in a meaningful Christian-Jewish dialogue.
"...This is not an assault or an attack against anti-Semitism. It is a scholar's heartfelt plea for Jews and Christians to talk to each other with candor, and it is presented against the background of the Holocaust and the still-extant anti-Semitism found in the Christian community.—*The Jewish Week*
0-87052-50903 $15.95 hc $8.95 pb

HOW TO BE JEWISH *by David Gross*
"This straightforward explanation provides a primer on Judaism for the layman who seeks to increase his knowledge of Jewish heritage, holidays, beliefs, and even language."—*The Jewish Week*
0-87052-069-5 $7.95 pb

JUDAISM *by David Gross*
From chapters on "Ancient Origins" and "Belief in God" to those focusing on Judaism and the family, this book is a concise yet complete grounding in the Jewish religion. Includes a chronological history of Judaism.
0-87052-068-7 $14.95 hc
0-7818-0237-7 $11.95 pb

ADDITIONAL TITLES OF JEWISH INTEREST

JEWS IN OLD CHINA *by Sidney Shapiro*
0-87052-553-0 $8.95 pb

WARS OF THE JEWS *by Rosenthal and Mozesom*
0-87052-786-X $16.95 hc

WANDERING JEW *by E. Sue*
0-94662-6332 $22.50 pb

YIDDISH-ENGLISH/ENGLISH-YIDDISH DICTIONARY *by D. Gross*
0-87052-969-2 $7.95 pb

All prices subject to change.

Order directly from HIPPOCRENE BOOKS by sending a check or mail order for the price of the book, plus $4.00 shipping and handling for the first book, and $.50 for each additional book to: HIPPOCRENE BOOKS, 171 MADISON AVE., NEW YORK, NY 10016

HIPPOCRENE JUDAICA BOOKS

POLAND'S JEWISH HERITAGE *by Joram Kagan*
This new guide is a must-have for Jewish travelers to Poland, a country which had the second largest Jewish community in the world prior to World War II. The guide includes historical background, as well as chronological tables showing the history of Polish Jewry. A hundred maps and photos complement the guide's detailed lists of synagogues, cemeteries and other places of Jewish heritage.
0-87052-991-9 $16.95

GLASSMAKERS: An Odyssey of the Jews *by Samuel Kurinsky*
The only work of its kind on the topic of glassmaking, it is fascinating reading for those interested in early Judaica lore.
"Eight years of research, begun in Venice and followed back into the archaeological digs of the Near East, show that glassmaking was an ancient art of the Jews which they carried with them as they moved from one area to another. Eleven chapters packed with facts and stories are a wonderful introduction to the history of ancient civilizations and their connections to the present."
—*Association of Jewish Libraries Newsletter*
32 photos
0-87052-901-3 $29.50

ENGLISH-HEBREW/HEBREW-ENGLISH DICTIONARY
by David Gross
7,000 transliterated, Romanized entries followed by helpful hints on pronunciation make up this compact dictionary.
"Ideal for those planning to visit Israel or beginning conversational Hebrew...useful phrases and maximum encouragement to start talking Hebrew."—*The Jewish Week*
"Beautifully arranged in a clear, concise type..."
—*Association of Jewish Libraries Newsletter*
0-87052-625-1 $7.95

FROM HIPPOCRENE

1,201 QUESTIONS AND ANSWERS ABOUT JUDAISM

David C. Gross

Now in its third edition, this book has distinguished itself as one of our bestselling Judaica books of all times and was a Book-of-the-Month Club selection. Filled with fun and fascinating facts, the former two editions received rave reviews.
328 pages
0-7818-0050-1 $11.95 pb

"Ideal for busy people seeking ready answers on the basic questions....the amount of information packed into this one volume is amazing..."
—Rabbi Alexander Shindler, Pres., Union of Hebrew Congregations

"A kaleidoscopic vision of the rich heritage of Judaism."
—Rabbi Norman Lamm, Pres., Yeshiva University

All prices subject to change.
Order directly from HIPPOCRENE BOOKS by sending a check or money order for the price of the book, plus $4.00 shipping and handling for the first book, and $.50 for each additional book to: HIPPOCRENE BOOKS, 171 MADISON AVE., NEW YORK, NY 10016